To Geeta and Kilu
for having shown me the joys of wondering,
for having gifted me with a childhood that was never theirs,
...
for having given me courage to seek Truth and Beauty.
It is to them that I dedicate the work of my life.

ACKNOWLEDGMENTS

It is difficult to compress in a few lines one's gratitude to a number of people who have had any bearing on this dissertation. I want to thank Dr. Shamkant Navathe, with whom I have worked for five years, for opening many opportunities to me and being one of the most flexible and understanding advisors that one can have. I want to thank Manuel Bermudez for teaching me denotational semantics and all that I know about programming languages. I spent two great years working with Howard Beck on the CANDIDE project, during which period I learned much. The rudiments of Voltaire lay in a "mercurial" late night discussion with Stephan Grill over beer.

It has always been a joy to discuss the meaning of life, the universe, ..., and 42 with Dr. Principé; he has shown me that it is possible to learn as many things in one's life as one cares to. I would also like to thank Drs. Chakravarthy, Lam and Su for many illuminating discussions on Voltaire and other topics. It would be difficult to recount the various interactions with past and present students who have shared the Database Center as a superlative work place. But, I should like to thank Rahim Yaseen, who taught me more about Unix and other systems oriented concepts.

Without Sharon Grant, the Database Center could not have been the great place that it is. She manages it with dedication, care and a smile. Of course, she also provides M&Ms. Working late nights was made much bearable by "short" coffee breaks with Niranjan Mayya and Ravi Malladi, which occasionally got extended to Cedar Key!

TABLE OF CONTENTS

Abstract of Dissertation
Presented to the Graduate School of the University of Florida
in Partial Fulfillment of the Requirements for the
Degree of Doctor of Philosophy

VOLTAIRE: A DATABASE PROGRAMMING ENVIRONMENT WITH A SINGLE EXECUTION MODEL FOR EVALUATING QUERIES, SATISFYING CONSTRAINTS AND COMPUTING FUNCTIONS

By

Sunit Gala

December 1991

Chairman: Shamkant B. Navathe
Major Department: Electrical Engineering

In this thesis we present Voltaire, which is a set-oriented, imperative database programming language. The set expressions in the language are conducive to data intensive programming while maintaining a certain amount of efficiency by espousing the imperative paradigm. The language and its semantics are defined in a modular but additive fashion, which facilitates some measure of bootstrapping. We further argue that such an implementation model is desirable, since it provides a single execution model for evaluating queries, satisfying constraints and computing functions.

The system provides automatic integrity enforcement in a lazy evaluation mode. Functions are effectively computed as the result of integrity enforcement. This is because we consider constraints as a sequence of commands to be evaluated or satisfied in the specified order. There are no arbitrary restrictions on the persistence of values—even functions can have a persistent extent. Further, the query language incorporates functions by providing access to the persistent extent of a function or by allowing an actual function call. Also, the compiler can exploit conventional algebraic techniques for query optimization.

The data definition (or type) facility is similar to what might be found in most semantic data models and is conducive to sharing heterogeneous records. We have defined a type algebra that incorporates structure, extent and behavior by providing an extensional semantics for the behavior. We also attempt to define a denotational semantics for the Voltaire language and environment.

We believe that Voltaire is a suitable language for data intensive programming, and is a reasonable compromise between a database system and a programming language.

CHAPTER 1
DATABASE PROGRAMMING LANGUAGES

1.1 Introduction

In today's typical organization, a large proportion of software applications are in fact database applications and are developed at considerable cost. The development of these applications is usually performed using two distinct, incompatible languages: one for data manipulation and one for programming the application. For example, COBOL is often used as the "host" programming language, in which SQL data manipulation statements are embedded.

This is the case in most business applications which constitute the largest consumers of database technology. A typical database management system consists of a data definition language (DDL) and a data manipulation language (DML) [25]. The DDL defines the database structure and hence constitutes the structural component, whereas the DML consists of a query sublanguage (i.e., retrieval operators) and update operators. For example, in a relational database, sets of relations and various integrity constraints form the structural component or DDL, while the query language (QL) is based on the relational calculus or algebra. Further, the relational QL is set–oriented and declarative in nature. Thus, embedding declarative DML statements in an imperative host language inevitably leads to a paradigm mismatch between the languages.

The application developer often spends inordinate amounts of time and energy overcoming these incompatibilities. The incompatibilities are not just conceptual, but physical as well. For example, sharing of symbol space and work space between the embedded and host languages creates challenges for implementation. Thus, Database Programming Languages (DBPLs) have been proposed to alleviate this problem, by integrating programming language constructs and database constructs into a single language, (see, for example, [1, 3, 4, 6, 8, 9, 23, 26, 28, 34, 37, 41, 43, 44, 48, 51, 52]).

There are some important issues concerning the design of database programming languages [5, 7, 12, 16]. Perhaps the most difficult issue stems from the fact that data modeling (and knowledge representation) enterprises are ontologic in nature, in contrast to traditional programming. This means that the role of a data model is to faithfully capture the semantics of some real world entity without worrying about the actual data structures with which to implement the given entity. On the other hand, the role of a rich type system in a traditional programming language is to allow the user to choose a data structure which will lead to the most efficient implementation of the application in question. Designing a DBPL necessarily entails the merging of certain incompatible features of a database system and programming language. Thus, the type system of a programming language must be elevated to match the ontologic properties of a data model to enhance the computational expressibility of the resulting DBPL. Unfortunately, a uniform treatment of types, behavior, extent and classes is a non-trivial problem. An important reason for this seems to be that a type definition usually does not account for the extent of a type [16, 5, 15] whereas a database class definition does provide a semantic description of its extent (i.e., the closed world assumption). Further, it is important that the type system provide structures (such as classes) for representing sets of similar, but possibly heterogeneous structures (such as records or instances).

We would also like to emphasize that many proposed DBPLs do not provide a truly integrated computing paradigm. For example, they do not provide a homogeneous treatment of object (type or class) manipulation and function (procedure or method) specification. This lack of homogeneity stems from the fact that there are three sublanguages that form a single DBPL. These sublanguages are for data definition to specify object types, data manipulation to compute a restricted class of queries, and function specification for making arbitrary computations. It is important to note that in many existing DBPLs (an exception being the embedding of relational systems within logic languages), the three sublanguages are orthogonal, i.e., there tends to be no interleaving among programming language constructs, data manipulation constructs, and data definition constructs. Instead, the three sublanguages are merely "appended" to each other, which results in a DBPL lacking a truly integrated paradigm. However, appending languages in this manner is still a vast improvement over embedding queries in a host language (such as SQL in COBOL).

We shall briefly enumerate some issues that lead to conflicts when designing a database programming language:

1. Set–oriented manipulation primitives versus record-oriented programming primitives.

2. Declarative query language versus imperative programming language.

3. Ability to define a theory of types which accounts for extent as well as behavior involves certain compromises:

   (a) a type theory must be able to clearly define when one class is a subclass of another, and when a database object belongs to a given class;

   (b) static versus dynamic type checking;

   (c) polymorphism versus efficiency;

   (d) ability to deal with heterogeneous records or objects;

4. Uniform persistence for all objects independent of their type versus efficient retrieval from secondary storage.

5. Ability to define the notion of a transaction.

6. Ability to provide referential transparency between objects in main memory and those in secondary storage.

1.2 Scope of this Dissertation

In this dissertation we present Voltaire, a set-oriented, imperative database programming language. The set expressions in the language are conducive to data intensive programming while maintaining a certain amount of efficiency by subscribing to the imperative paradigm. The language and its semantics are defined in a modular but additive fashion, which facilitates a bootstrapped implementation. We further argue that such an implementation model is desirable. The data definition (or type) facility is similar to what might be found in most semantic data models and is conducive to sharing heterogeneous records. The query language provides uniform access to sets of instances as well as functions. Also, the compiler can exploit conventional algebraic techniques for query optimization. The system provides automatic integrity enforcement (up to a certain degree). Functions are effectively computed as the result of integrity enforcement. This is because we consider constraints as a sequence of commands to be evaluated or satisfied in the specified order. Further, there are no arbitrary restrictions on the persistence of values—even functions can have a persistent extent.

We view Voltaire as an experiment to provide a language facility to manipulate sets of associative data. Our set expressions are superficially similar to those in SETL [49], thus reducing certain paradigm mismatch problems with record-oriented languages. The design of our language in general and our inheritance and data declaration scheme, in particular, strongly reflect the database notion that a class denotes a set of instances that belong to it. We provide the following functionality in Voltaire:

1. a data definition facility similar to what might be found in most semantic data models [30],
2. a query language which provides uniform access to sets of instances as well as functions [7],
3. automatic constraint management (up to a certain degree), for reasonably expressive constraints [40], and
4. ability to specify and compute arbitrary functions.

The first three features are based on the core functionality that a typical DBMS must provide. Arbitrary functions are then computed under the control of the DBMS. All of the above functionality is provided by a single execution model, which reflects a bootstrapped implementation (see Figure 1.1c). Further, there are no arbitrary restrictions on the persistence of values. We shall not be dealing with other important issues such as concurrency, transaction management, recovery or active database management (essential for efficient integrity enforcement). The main contributions of this dissertation can be summarized as follows:

1. define a semantics for types, incorporating extent and behavior, that emphasizes the notion that a class (or type) denotes a set of objects,
2. allow a set of heterogeneous records (objects) to belong to a single class to facilitate sharing of data,

3. alleviate the paradigm mismatch between record-oriented and set-oriented primitives for manipulating associative data within the language by means of type coercion,

4. provide a modicum of efficiency by subscribing to the imperative paradigm within a set-oriented language, and

5. provide a single model of execution for evaluating queries, enforcing constraints and computing functions, by designing a language that facilitates some measure of bootstrapping.

The rest of this dissertation is organized as follows. In the remainder of chapter 1, we list some general design criteria for database programming languages and discuss previous research. Then in chapter 2, we give a brief overview of the design rationale of Voltaire and some of its features. In chapter 3, we describe the data definition facility in Voltaire along with update operators and give a formal semantics of the type model used in the language. In chapter 4, we describe the features of the query sublanguage with the help of examples and also outline possible execution strategies. In chapter 5, the constraint specification sublanguage is described. In chapter 6, we first introduce the basic structure of functions in Voltaire and give a number of examples. Then we explain how the notion of temporary instance creation provides an operational means for giving an equivalent semantics to classes and functions in the run-time environment. This is followed by a theoretical explanation of why classes and functions can have an equivalent semantics and some implications thereof. In chapter 7, we first describe how a user can interact with the Voltaire environment, followed by a denotational semantics of the language. Finally, we summarize our conclusions and the main contributions of this dissertation, as well as define future research goals in chapter 8.

1.3 Some Design Criteria for DBPLs

Here we discuss the implications of merging the database and programming language cultures, which have traditionally been divergent. We feel that these issues discussed elsewhere [5, 7, 12, 16] have been predominantly viewed from a programming language standpoint. We must first note that the primary function of a database management system (DBMS) is to provide a persistent store of bulk data structures for efficiently processing transactions on sets of such data.

More traditional application domains are data intensive, that is, the application tends to have a large volume of instances or records, and relatively fewer types or classes. Therefore, it is conceivable that existing data models are extended to provide advanced functionality such as the ability to compute arbitrary functions or active data management [39, 46, 55]. The ability to define and handle various kinds of transactions is crucial in these applications. In contrast, newer application areas such as CAD/CAM or CASE are computation intensive; that is, they tend to have a large number of types or classes, each class having few instances, but requiring some database functionality. It may be more expeditious to extend a given programming language such that it provides DBMS-like functionality [1, 44, 48, 52]. Hence, it seems that before designing a DBPL, the expected application domain should be known, since it is rather difficult (however desirable it may be) to design a system which can solve all problems. Most DBPLs seem to have taken the second option with certain exceptions. Some of these are relational systems embedded within logic and procedural languages [28, 34, 36, 48] and other systems such as [33, 52]. There is a third class of DBPLs which are designed from scratch and address specific issues. These languages tend to be more experimental in nature.

We now attempt to analyze the effects of both the above options on various features that a DBPL may have.

1.3.1 Semantic Data Model versus Persistent Abstract Data Types

A semantic data model rigidly defines the structure of objects (or instances) which reside in a persistent store, and classes which describe these objects. Type constructors can only be used to define the domain of values which various attributes of a given object can assume. This means that new classes cannot be defined (or constructed) by applying type constructors to existing types; such manipulation is allowed only in the query language. In contrast, there are no such restrictions on type constructors with an abstract data type. However, with the abstract data type approach, the database administrator must determine the most suitable data types and structures for the application at hand, and also write a set of create, update, delete and retrieve routines for each such structure. This is usually not considered a satisfactory situation in the database culture, primarily because it violates the principle of data independence. A partial remedy may be to distinguish between persistent and non-persistent data types, so that generic operators for manipulating the persistent objects can be efficiently implemented. But then this violates the principle of uniform persistence, i.e., persistence should be orthogonal to type [5]. Therefore, choosing a rigid data model implies efficient access to the persistent store but a lack of a rich typing mechanism, whereas the second option implies inefficient access to the secondary store but a rich typing mechanism and extensibility.

We would like to emphasize that persistent programming languages are not database programming languages. This is because when a programming language is extended to provide persistence, its type theory is usually not appropriately extended.

That is, such type systems are often unable to answer the following questions in a clear fashion:

1. when is one class (type) a subclass (subtype) of another?
2. when is an object (instance or record) a member of the domain of a given class (or type)?

Another problem with these type systems is that they often do not provide transparency between persistent and transient objects, that is, a separate set of operators is defined for persistent set of objects. Hence, we believe that persistent versions of languages such as C++, Smalltalk or Ada cannot be classified as DBPLs, but should be considered as intermediate (albeit important) steps towards one.

1.3.2 Type Checking

The general consensus here seems to be that the language should be strongly typed, though some obviously convenient overloading may be allowed [5]. There also seems to be a consensus that type checking should be static as far as possible. This would minimize run-time errors thus saving on the transaction processing overhead (catching a run-time error late in the transaction may result in a number of *undo* operations). Static type checking can be difficult to achieve in highly polymorphic languages, though some progress has been reported [43, 54].

1.3.3 Ability to Manipulate Heterogeneous Sets

Type definitions in languages such as C++ do not account for the extent of the type. This contrasts with the database notion of a class, which denotes the set of all instances that belong to that class. There has been much recent work on defining type schemes which attempt to define the extent of a type [5, 15, 16, 18, 19, 54]. An important feature is the ability to manipulate sets of heterogeneous data. For example, the language Machiavelli [43] defines a type discipline in which it is possible to write polymorphic functions, which may operate on sets of different kinds. However, a particular execution of the function may only operate on a set whose elements belong to a single kind.

1.3.4 Ability to Share Data

The ability to share data (heterogeneous or otherwise) should be an important property of a database programming environment. Sharing can occur in three ways:

1. A single schema can describe multiple databases. For example, a chain of stores can have a single schema to describe the inventory at all of its locations.

2. A single database can have multiple schemas describing it (unlike views). For example, a plant manager and plant engineer can have two different schemas emphasizing different aspects of the same CAM database.

3. Multiple users may wish to share a given database (possibly viewed through different schemas).

1.3.5 Data versus Functions

Since independent applications access the same shared data under the control of a DBMS, the focus of a DBMS is on the data. On the other hand, the focus in a programming language is on the application itself, and the data types are simply a mechanism for efficient implementation of the application. This traditional separation of data from function leads to a very fundamental conflict when designing a DBPL, having implications on constraint management, ad hoc querying and transaction processing. For example, let us examine the implications on an application independent (i.e., ad hoc) query mechanism. Since functions (or methods or procedures) can be used to generate derived attributes, it becomes necessary to be able to query them [7]. Consider the class *person* with attributes ***birthdate*** and ***age*** and a function called ***compute_age*** which computes the age of a person given his/her birth date and the current date. The query reference ***person.age*** should automatically trigger the ***compute_age*** function. Alternately, the language should allow the query reference ***person.compute_age***. Ideally, the DBPL should allow functions to be accessed in a fashion similar to that of other objects.

1.3.6 Database Integrity

The importance of database integrity should be established for the given application area, and also it should be decided as to how much of the burden for maintaining this integrity can be placed on the application programmer before designing a DBPL. Typically, in traditional database systems, integrity is enforced by application programs. However, enforcing integrity constraints is considered an important database function, which should be handled by the DBMS itself. Some recent solutions to this problem have been discussed in the area of active databases [39, 40]. When dealing with complex objects, the DBMS must at least be capable of maintaining referential integrity. It is relatively difficult to define a theory of types that also takes into account the extent of the type in persistent store, since the user has complete freedom to define any arbitrary type. This makes it even more difficult to identify and enforce integrity constraints. The fundamental conflict here is that a database associates constraints with objects (i.e., automatic triggering of constraints when an object is created, updated or deleted), whereas in a programming language, constraints are embedded in the procedure and therefore cannot be triggered automatically. Much recent work on constraint management is reported in the active database literature [21, 39, 46, 55]. This would also lead to a more efficient transaction management, since a user-defined procedure for maintaining integrity can have arbitrary side effects, thus making it impossible to automatically determine which constraints will be violated. However, it is not yet clear how the notion of an active database can be merged with a programming language to design a DBPL.

1.3.7 Role of the Query Language

A database user usually needs to retrieve or otherwise operate on sets of similar valued objects defined by various classes. The query language is the mechanism that allows the user to specify a restricted class of computations to operate on such sets. It usually allows only restricted computations so as to maximize efficiency. The considerations for optimizing a query processor are significantly different from those in programming languages, which typically operate on one object at a time in virtual memory. Query optimizers rely heavily on clustering information on the disk, indexing, caching, and the algebraic properties of the primitive operators provided by the query language. Ideally, one would want to augment the computing power of a query language by making it a "proper" subset of the programming language. (By proper subset we mean that by removing all querying primitives from the DBPL, it would be rendered Turing incomplete.) In this scenario, it would be possible to make arbitrary computations efficiently as well as to evaluate ad hoc queries. But it should be pointed out here that if the DBPL were to have a very rich type system where the persistent bulk data are of various different types, then query optimization becomes too complex to be effective. This is because each bulk data type would have its own associated optimization technique. Additionally, if the bulk data types are vastly different from each other, then it can be very difficult to meaningfully overload the query language primitives. For instance, it might be difficult to define a single "join" operator for relations in first normal form and user-defined complex objects in a non-relational format. After all, the notion of uniform persistence should quite naturally be extended to the notion that the query language should be uniform (i.e., have a small set of operations that apply uniformly across) for all data types. This might be possible only in a language whose type system is highly polymorphic, and even if so, would be achieved only at the expense of sacrificing efficiency. Some work towards this end is reported in [22, 35, 43, 50, 53, 56].

1.3.8 Implementation Strategies

Traditional database functionality such as concurrency, locking and transaction management facilitate data sharing. Such functionality is based on the notion that a class denotes the set of instances that belong to it. Thus, it seems important that a database programming language emphasize data rather than function.[1] Figure 1.1 shows some possible implementation strategies—Figure 1.1a simply depicts a classical situation where DML statements are embedded in some host language. It is perhaps fair to say that Figure 1.1b depicts a typical implementation of the newer generation of database systems. Such implementations are in agreement with some recent work on extensible systems [10, 20]. From the application programmer's point of view, Figures 1.1b and 1.1c are functionally equivalent. However, we believe that Figure 1.1c is a cleaner and more desirable implementation model because:

1. it is possible for syntactic structures to be shared without harmfully overloading their semantics,
2. it would be easier to bootstrap such a system,
3. it would lead towards a smaller, integrated language, and
4. it would reduce communication overhead between the various modules.

[1]This is in contradistinction to functional data models such as DAPLEX [51] or PDM [38].

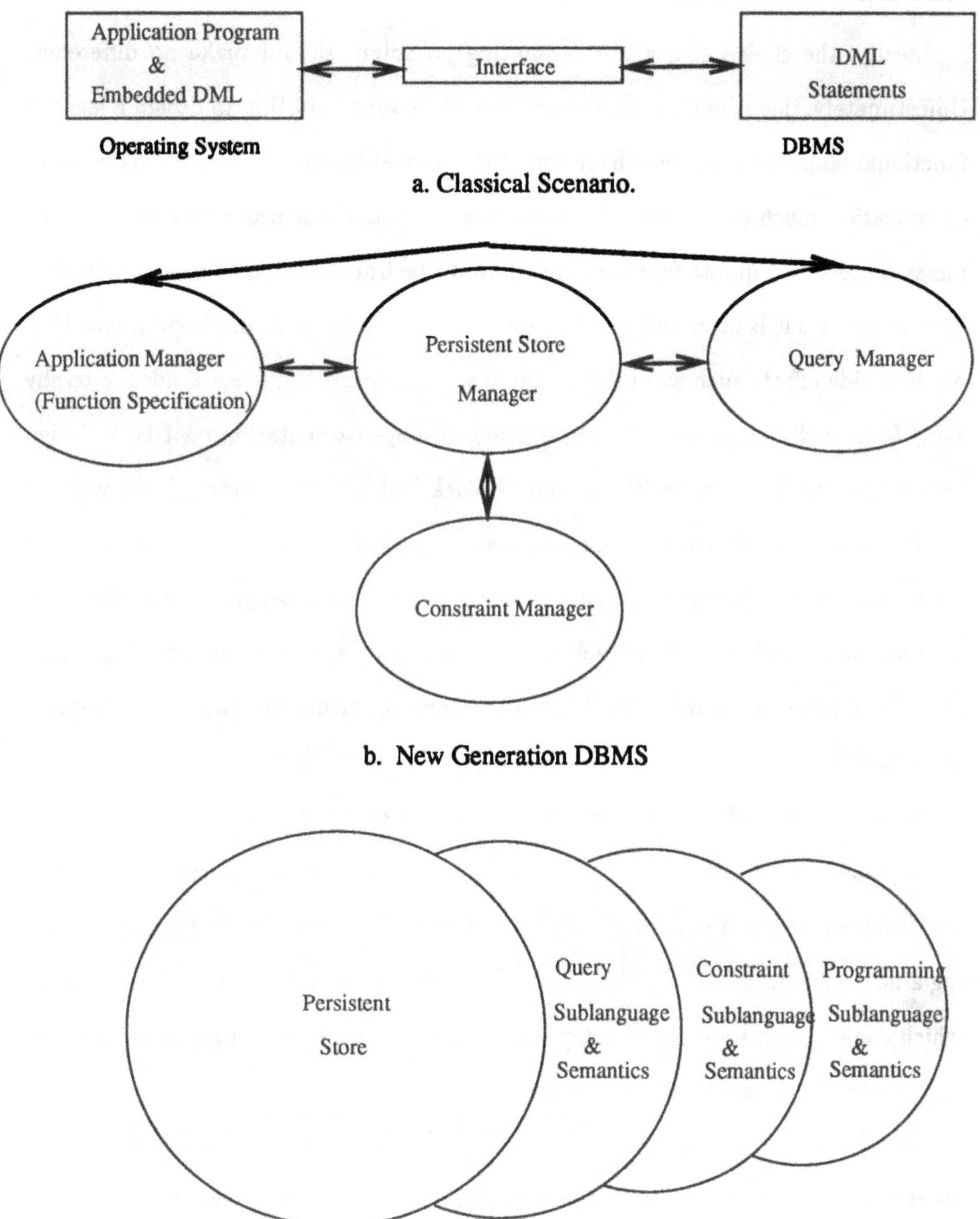

Figure 1.1. Implementation Strategies

1.3.9 Choice of Computing Paradigm

Ideally, the choice of a given computing paradigm should make no difference. Unfortunately, this is not the case in practice. It is very tempting to design a logic or functional language since they have sound theoretical bases. This would make query optimization much easier, but the semantics of transaction processing can become messy because all update functions may have to be implemented as meta-predicates. This is because it is often difficult to provide a formal description of operations that produce side effects such as updates. Besides, users seem to have a tendency to shy away from such languages. The implications of object-orientation on DBPL design have been well discussed in Bloom and Zdonick [12] and Bancilhon [7] and will not be discussed here. Procedural languages such as COBOL or C or Pascal have the main advantage of being rather popular among application programmers. However, they are considered to be "low-level" and therefore not expressive enough. Also, most procedural languages have virtually no set processing primitives (with the exception of COBOL).

However, from a database perspective, we feel that the destructive assignment operator causes the most problems. In a truly integrated DBPL environment [5] with uniform persistence, it is difficult to prevent the user from (even accidentally) assigning a new value to a field. In effect, such an assignment is an update to the database which could spawn potentially many subtransactions for checking constraints before the assignment operation could be committed and the next command executed. (This is in addition to the usual problems such as garbage collection and dangling references caused by destructive assignment.) The destructive assignment operator is the bête noire of automatic side-effect detection and constraint management. Unfortunately, the destructive assignment operator is necessary to achieve efficiency and better performance.

Regardless of which design strategy or language paradigm is chosen, one obvious pitfall to avoid is the PL/1 syndrome.[2] Many DBPLs that are the result of three orthogonal sublanguages being appended to each other (see section 1.1) are also victims (though to a much lesser degree) of the PL/1 syndrome. For instance, it is better to provide different kinds of users with various library functions, rather than incorporating language constructs for everything. Since one of the design goals of a DBPL is to cater to a larger variety of users, the environment should provide default primitives for each functionality which can be easily superseded by the user.

1.4 Previous Research

Most DBPLs described in the literature fall into three main design options:

1. Embed a given data model in some programming language, e.g., Pascal/R [48], Modula/R [34], ADAPLEX [52], O_2 [35], Gemstone [23].

2. Provide persistence to a programming language (some languages also provide set manipulation primitives), e.g., PS-Algol [6], ODE [1], ONTOS [44].

3. Design a new system from scratch, e.g., TAXIS [41], Galileo [3], Machiavelli [43]. Voltaire falls in this category. TAXIS offers elaborate exception handling and meta-data definition capabilities, while the other two have polymorphic type systems based on ML [29]. Galileo is an expression-oriented language, thus eliminating the need for an explicit query language. Machiavelli is a functional

[2]The PL/1 syndrome is a design pitfall in which an arbitrarily large number of constructs are provided. This in turn leads to a large and unwieldy language which is difficult to implement or learn.

language which explicitly addresses the type versus class issue and the ability to manipulate sets of heterogeneous elements.

The first class of languages is engineered to provide a relatively clean interface between the record-oriented programming language primitives and set manipulation primitives for the underlying data model. Another important class of such languages are relational systems embedded within logic languages [27]. However, the main problem with these languages is that a certain amount of paradigm mismatch remains. For example, in Pascal/R, Pascal is an imperative language whereas the relational model and its query language are declarative.

In the second class of languages, we have PS-Algol, which provides a persistent store for all types in Algol. On the other hand, ODE and ONTOS are extensions of C++, in which the only persistent structures are C++ classes. The problem with these languages is that they have not addressed the type versus class issues. When extending these languages with persistence, their type systems are not appropriately extended. That is, the type systems of these extended languages are unable to answer one or both of the following questions:

1. when is one class (type) a subclass (subtype) of another?

2. when is an object (instance or record) a member of the domain of a given class (or type)?

In the third class of languages, to which Voltaire belongs, TAXIS is one of the earliest efforts. It is a record-oriented language with a very elaborate exception handling mechanism. It provides arbitrary levels of meta-classes, and transactions and exceptions can be organized into a taxonomy. The language relied heavily on associative access by means of a dot operator. However, it did not have set manipulation primitives, and constraints could be satisfied only by means of defining appropriate transactions and handling exceptions. Also, TAXIS classes are derived mainly from semantic networks rather than a typical type system [19]. In Voltaire, we provide a similar dot operator for associative access, as well as set manipulation primitives and automatic constraint management. Further, the type system is well-defined.

Galileo is an expression-oriented language with an ML-style type discipline. In such languages, expressions are evaluated directly; there is no need to write a function (or query) and then compile it before executing it. Therefore, it eliminates the need for a separate query language. A main design goal was to view Galileo as a conceptual design tool. Unlike Voltaire, it offers no automatic constraint management. Although Voltaire is not expression-oriented, we do not need a separate query language (largely due to its bootstrapped design).

Machiavelli is a functional language with an ML-style type discipline. An important aspect of its polymorphism is an underlying algebra of sets based on the homomorphic extension operator [17]. It also defines a coherent type theory which can deal with sets of heterogeneous records. Unlike Voltaire, a notion of persistence is still be to be defined, and it does not support automatic constraint management. Like Machiavelli, we have an underlying algebra of sets based on the homomorphic extension operator. An important difference is that a unique identifier (and optionally, the name of the class) is automatically a part of any instance created in the system.

By contrast, O_2 defines a theory of types based on Cardelli [18]. The semantics of behavior (i.e., methods) is captured by defining a signature (which is a set of functions attached to a class or type). The O_2 data model is embedded within C and Basic. The semantics of our type system is based on that of O_2 with two main differences:

1. we support multiple inheritance, and

2. we model behavior by giving it an entirely extensional interpretation, rather than as a signature.

Thus, the design of Voltaire was heavily influenced by Machiavelli, TAXIS and O_2. Further, none of these languages provide a means to share data as described in section 1.3.4.

CHAPTER 2
AN OVERVIEW OF VOLTAIRE

While there are a number of issues governing the design of a database programming language, we have chosen to address only a few of them. The Voltaire environment is intended to be used as a vehicle in which a user can efficiently define his or her application with ease. The applications are expected to be data intensive, as opposed to computation intensive. An environment that is easy to use can result when the user need only focus on the specification of the application, rather than worry about dealing with paradigm mismatch problems between the host programming language and the DDL/DML (as discussed in the previous chapter). Thus, our primary goal is to provide the user with a truly integrated paradigm for data intensive computing. We achieve this by providing a single model of execution for evaluating queries, enforcing constraints and computing functions, by designing a language that facilitates a bootstrapped implementation. Further, we define an extensional semantics for behavior in our type theory, thereby giving an equivalent semantics to classes and functions. Thus, a function is computed as the result of constraint satisfaction. We first present the design rationale of Voltaire, followed by a brief overview of its various programming constructs.

2.1 Design Rationale of Voltaire

The basic structure of a query expression is as shown below:

<Query> ::= { <Dot_Expr> "|" <Bool> }

<Bool> ::= $< E_1 >$ **and** $< E_2 > \mid \cdots \mid < E_1 > < rel - op > < E_2 > \mid$

<E> ::= <Reg_Expr> | <Query> | <Dot_Expr>

<Dot_Expr> ::= <Identifier> | <Identifier>.<Dot_Expr>

A query consists of associative set expressions (see chapter 4). The user specifies a path (or subgraph) of interest on the LHS of the vertical bar, and boolean predicates for selection conditions on the RHS of the vertical bar. This path of interest denotes the context of the set expression within which certain boolean conditions must hold true. The further defines the scope of identifiers. A simple context can be specified by using a dot expression such as *Student.Course.Dept.* As an example, consider the query {Student.name | Student.Course.c# > 6000 **and** Student.advisor **in** Faculty}. The syntactic category <E> denotes expressions which are simple extensions to terms and factors found in most languages such as Pascal. A query can contain embedded subqueries since a query is a kind of expression, and <Bool> consists of expressions.

Boolean expressions have the usual **and, or, not** operators, quantifiers and relational expressions of the form < E_1 > <rel-op> < E_2 >. Thus, a constraint is of the form:

<Constraint> ::= **if** <Bool> **then** <Consequent>

The issue is to define the syntactic category <Consequent>:

1. without introducing further syntactic categories, and
2. without overloading the semantics of existing structures in an unnatural fashion.

This can be resolved by overloading the equality operator such that two conditions arise. If both the RHS and LHS are bound, then satisfiability is checked. If the LHS of the equality operator is unbound, then an assignment (or, more appropriately, a binding) takes place. Thus, <Consequent> ::= <Bool>. If these boolean conditions are chosen to be simple propositions, then satisfiability is NP-complete (due to the satisfiability problem), and the order in which constraints appear is insignificant. But such a choice would be inadequate for the following reasons:

1. lack of expressive power,

2. computational overhead due to insignificance in the order of constraints,

3. it raises the issue of how to blend such a semantics into a programming language that is not based on theorem proving techniques (such as resolution).

By taking a rather operational view in which the order of constraints is significant, we can avoid the above problems. Also, we can blend constraints into a set-oriented yet imperative programming language. A program can then be viewed as a sequence of constraints and other commands:

<Program> ::= <Sequence>+

<Sequence> ::= <Constraint> | <Command>

The category <Command> may consist of operators with side effects such as updates or input-output or other convenient constructs such as an iterator. Given the above interpretation, there is no *a priori* reason why a command cannot be a kind of consequent as well, i.e., <Consequent> ::= <Bool> | <Command>. Constraints are no longer viewed as mere pre- and post-conditions on the state of a computation, but rather as conditions that must hold true at arbitrarily specified points in a computation. This scheme is fairly general—consider the following:

<Constraint> ::= **if** <Antecedent> **then** <Consequent>

The antecedent of a constraint can also be events such as updates or retrieves, or exceptions. These issues are important in active database management [13, 21, 39, 40]. Thus, <Antecedent> ::= <Bool> | <Event> | <Exception>.

The main limitation of this operational interpretation is that constraints cannot be automatically propagated, other than what has been explicitly programmed by a user. For example, the user would have to write a rule such that if any employee is deleted, then delete all dependents of such an employee. If such rules are omitted in the definition of a given class, then the database may result in an inconsistent state. However, by adopting a lazy evaluation strategy, consistent data can be guaranteed as the result of evaluating an expression[1] (recall that a query is only one kind of expression). The above discussion is based on the implicit assumption that expressions can be evaluated against a persistent store, i.e., a database. We believe that the above formulation leads towards a bootstrapped implementation.

Other issues that we chose to address in the design of Voltaire with respect to the issues outlined in section 1.3 are:

1. We define an object-based data model (or type system) that accounts for both extent and behavior, and facilitates manipulation of heterogeneous records and sharing of data. Further, operators defined in the language are transparent to the persistence or non-persistence of objects. The set-oriented expressions can be statically checked for type errors.

2. We alleviate the paradigm mismatch problem between record- and set-oriented paradigms by designing a language based on set expressions, by employing implicit type coercion, and some obvious operator overloading.

3. We provide a limited form of automatic constraint management. The query language can uniformly access objects and functions.

To make our discussion more concrete, we shall briefly present an introductory example of data definition, constraints and functions written in Voltaire in section 2.3.

[1]This is precisely the view taken by Jagadish [31].

We shall adopt the following convention in all subsequent chapters. All identifiers for class names will begin with a capital letter, attribute names with a small letter and reserved words in bold face. In normal text, all identifiers will be italicized, except for reserved words.

2.2 A Quick Glance of Voltaire

Voltaire supports a number of features and abstraction mechanisms for modeling the data as well the application. We first list the abstractions for database modeling:

1. *Classes:* A class is a set of instances or objects being modeled, such that these objects share certain common characteristics. The name of a class denotes the objects currently existing in the database. There exists only one copy of the object in the database, though other objects may refer to it. A class definition consists of a sequence of <attribute_name, domain> pairs. An object can be a member of a class if it has at least those attributes defined in the class—thus an object can have additional attributes and belong to the class in question without the necessity for creating either a new subclass or an exception.

2. *Aggregation:* Objects belonging to classes are aggregates of heterogeneous components, having objects of other classes as components. Associations between various objects are represented as aggregations. An object is a sequence of <attribute_names, value> pairs.

3. *Generalization:* Voltaire supports a taxonomy of classes. Subclasses are derived from a class by adding more information to the class. Instances of a subclass also belong to its parent classes. Since we support multiple inheritance, an instance can have many parent classes or belong to a subclass which can have

many parent classes. Further, the type of the elements of a subclass is a subtype of the type of the elements of the parent class.

4. *Sharing:* The type system of Voltaire makes it possible for a given set of instances to be viewed or shared by more than one schema; or for a given schema to be able to define more than one set of instances (see section 1.3.4).

The Voltaire language also has the following characteristics:

1. Voltaire is a set-oriented but object-based language subscribing to the imperative paradigm of programming.

2. Expressions in Voltaire are a simple extension of terms and factors—the kind of expressions found in Pascal-like languages. An important extension is the set expression which returns a set of objects (values or instances) belonging to a given type. A simple set expression includes the dot operator which facilitates associative access.

3. The main control structure is the sequencing of commands or constraints. The language also provides conditionals, iterators, and recursive function call.

4. Every denotable value of the language possesses a type:

   (a) A type is a set of values sharing a set of common properties, together with a sequence of constraints which define the behavior of elements of a type.

   (b) The predefined types are *boolean, integer, real, string*, with the usual operators, the type *Nil*, which is a singleton set with the element *null*, and the type *Any*, of which all types are a subtype. Equality is defined for the type *Nil*, which is a subtype of all types defined in the schema.

(c) The type constructors *set* and *tuple* are available to define new types from predefined or previously defined types.

(d) A value of type τ_1 can be used as an argument to a function defined for values of type τ_2, if τ_1 is a subtype of τ_2. Since the subtype relation is a partial order, reverse substitution is not allowed.

5. It is a first order language. However, the extent of a function is a denotable value (which can also be persistent). Therefore, an element belonging to the extent of a function[2] can be embedded in data structures, passed as a parameter, or returned as a value. It should be noted that this approach is quite different from the one taken in higher order functional languages where the function itself is a denotable value.

6. Functions and classes in Voltaire have an equivalent semantics.

7. A given function is specified by the relationships between the input and output arguments of that function. These parameters form the attributes of the function (or class), and the relationships among them are expressed as a sequence of constraints. These relationships or constraints are rules for evaluating the function. Thus, the evaluation of a function can be seen as the result of sequential constraint satisfaction.

8. The Voltaire environment prompts the user for inputs and reports the result of computations in an interactive fashion. At this level of evaluation, the user can load a given schema (definitions of classes and functions) and a given database

[2]It is useful to think of an element of the extent of a function as a member of the graph of that function. The Voltaire system, however, treats it as an instance whose attributes (which correspond to the formal parameters of the function) are bound to denotable values, thus capturing pre- and post-computation information.

(a set of instances). Alternately, a new schema can be defined and a new database created. Further, one can evaluate set expressions (which, effectively, are queries) or execute functions.

2.3 An Introductory Example

We give below a simple example to illustrate the notion of sharing as defined in section 1.3.4. As mentioned there, a given schema can describe more than one consistent set of instances, and likewise, a given set of instances can be defined by more than one schema. Therefore, we define two simple schemas and two sets of instances.

Let Schema_1 be defined as follows:

```
class Employee defined
attributes
    name: string
    ss#: integer
    dept: Department
    manager: Employee
    salary: integer
Constraints

class Dept defined
attributes
    name: string
    location: string
    manager: Employee
    budget: integer
Constraints
    budget > sum {Employee.salary |
        Employee.dept.Dept.name = self .name };


class Incr_Salary function
attributes
    incr: integer
constraints
    for each x in Employee do
        {modify .x | salary = prev.salary + (prev.salary × incr) ÷ 100};
    enddo
```

Thus, Schema_1 consists of the two classes *Employee* and *Dept* and the function *Incr_Salary*. A constraint is defined on the class *Dept* such that the budget of each

Dept should be greater than the sum of the salaries of all employees working in it. The argument of the **sum** operator is effectively a query, in which **self** denotes the currently active instance of the class *Dept*. The function *Incr_Salary* increases the salary of each employee in the database by a given percentage. The dot expression **prev**.*salary* denotes the older value of salary. The command in the body of the **for** loop could have been alternately written as:

salary := salary + (salary × incr) ÷ 100;

Similarly, let Schema_2 be defined as follows:

```
class Employee defined              class Dept defined
attributes                          attributes
    name: string                        name: string
    manager: Employee                   manager: Employee
    salary: integer
Constraints                         Constraints
    self .salary < manager.salary
```

```
class Emps_in_Dept function
attributes
    dept_name: string
    dept_mgr: string
    emps_in_dept: set Employee
constraints
    dept_mgr = {Dept.manager | Dept.name = dept_name };
    emps_in_dept = {Employee | Employee.manager = dept_mgr; }
```

We again define *Employee* and *Dept* classes and a function *Emps_in_Dept* which determines all the employees working in a department given its name. The function could have been redefined without the identifier *dept_mgr* as follows:

```
emps_in_dept = {Employee | Employee.manager =
                              {Dept.manager | Dept.name = dept_name } };
```

Let the set of instances DB_1 be as follows:

instance joe **class** Employee
ss# = 123123123
name = "Joe"
dept = finance
manager = sally
salary = 60000

instance jim **class** Employee
ss# = 121212121
name = "Jim"
dept = production
manager = john
salary = 50000
car = "toyota"

instance harry **class** Employee
name = "Harry"
ss# = 111222333
dept = production
manager = harry
salary = 55000
spouse = sally

instance sally **class** Employee
name = "Sally"
ss# = 789789789
dept = finance
manager = sally
salary = 65000

instance production **class** Dept
name = "Production"
location = "austin"
manager = harry
budget = 6000000
employees = {jim, harry}

instance finance **class** Dept
name = "Finance"
location = "athens"
manager = sally
budget = 5550000

Note that the structures of the instances belonging to the classes *Employee* and *Dept* are different. For example, nothing is mentioned about spouses and cars in the class definition. Further, *sally* has a value for the attribute *manager* which points to itself. Such cyclic structures are legal in Voltaire. It means that Sally is her own manager. Similarly, let the set of instances DB_2 be as follows:

instance smith **class** Employee
name = "Smith"
manager = jack
salary = 45000
education = "M.S."

instance jill **class** Employee
name = "Jill"
manager = alice
salary = 54000
spouse = jack

instance jack **class** Employee
name = "Jack"
manager = jack
salary = 55000

instance alice **class** Employee
name = "Alice"
manager = alice
salary = 65000
dept = wonderland

instance wonderland **class** Dept
name = "Wonderland"
manager = alice
budget = **null**

We have defined a semantics for the type scheme that facilitates sharing of data (see section 3.4). Thus, $Schema_2$ can adequately define DB_1 and DB_2, since the type system will deduce that the corresponding structures are compatible. Similarly, DB_1 can be defined by $Schema_1$ and $Schema_2$.

CHAPTER 3
DATA DEFINITION

3.1 Classes and Instances

The data definition facility in Voltaire allows us to define classes and an inheritance hierarchy, as well as a database of instances. Depicted in Figure 3.1 is a schema graph that can be easily modeled in Voltaire. This schema is defined in appendix A. The purpose of this schema graph is to emphasize the associative nature of data in many applications. For example, the classes *Grad* and *Person* denoting the set of all graduate students and persons respectively in the universe of discourse can be defined as follows:

```
class Grad defined            class Person defined
superclasses Student          superclasses any
subclasses RA, TA             subclasses Student, Teacher
attributes                    attributes
    ss#: integer                  ss#: integer
    name: string                  name: string
    gpa: real
    major: Dept
    advisor: Faculty
    sections: set Section
```

The attributes *ss#* and *name* are inherited from the class *Person*; *gpa, major* and *sections* are inherited from *Student*, and therefore, need not have been repeated since *Person* was explicitly mentioned as a superclass in the definition of *Student*. Instances are characterized by a unique identifier, the set of classes to which the instance may belong, and the set of attribute value pairs. An instance may belong to one or more classes provided it satisfies all constraints attached to a given class and all of its superclasses. Some examples of instances are:

instance joe **class** Student
  ss# = 123123123
  name = "Joe"
  gpa = 3.5
  major = EE
  sections = s123, s234, s345

instance jim **class** Person
  ss# = 121212121
  name = "Jim"

instance john **class** Person
  ss# = 111222333
  name = "John"
  age = 35

instance jack **class** Person
  ss# = 789789789
  name = "Jack"
  salary = 12000

The first identifier "joe" after the keyword **instance** denotes a unique identifier for the instance in question. It belongs to the class *Student*. The value for *major* refers to an instance of class *Dept*, and that for *sections* is a set of unique identifiers belonging to the class *Section*. Further, notice that nothing was mentioned about *age* and *salary* in the definition of *Person*. However, since we have chosen to give an extensional semantics to class definitions similar to that in previous works [18, 35, 45], an instance may have an arity greater than that of the classes to which it may belong. This decision was made for the following reasons:

1. To allow a single schema to describe multiple databases.
2. To allow a single database to be described by multiple schemas.[1]
3. To prevent an unnecessary proliferation of classes such as *Person_with_age* or *Person_with_salary*, besides *Person*.
4. To provide a means to deal with incomplete information and exceptions.

[1]If a single database is described by more than one schema, then the class to which an instance belongs cannot be stored along with the instance. In such a case, the class of an instance must be inferred (or read from a pre-compiled table) when opening a database.

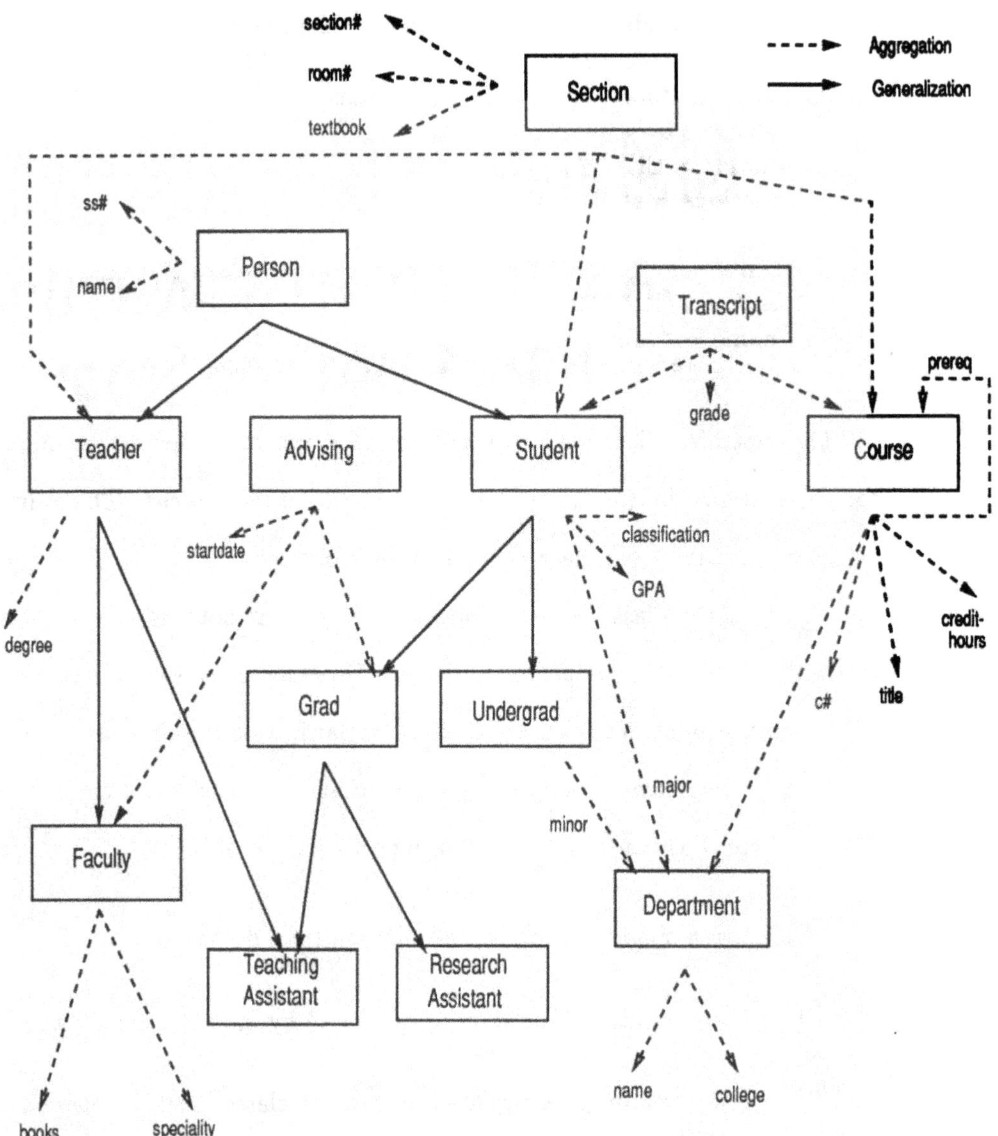

Figure 3.1. University Schema

Now, consider the following program segment:

```
s := { jim, john, jack };
for each x in s
    print x.name;
```

The reason why { jim, john, jack } is a valid structure is based on a simple extension of an idea described in Buneman and Ohori [17]. The idea is that one can define an ordering of database objects based on their information content, since a database object is a partial description of some real world entity. Thus, the instance (jim, ⟨ ss#: 121212121, name: "Jim"⟩) contains less information than (john, ⟨ ss#: 111222333, name: "John", age: 35⟩) and (jack, ⟨ ss#: 789789789, name: "Jack", salary: 12000 ⟩). If we were to assign types δ_1, δ_2 and δ_3, respectively, to these records, then one can define an ordering $\delta_2 \ll \delta_1$ and $\delta_3 \ll \delta_1$, where the ordering is $\ll$ based on the subtype relationship. Further, $\delta_1 = \sqcup\{\delta_1, \delta_2, \delta_3\}$, which can adequately define the type of {jim, john, jack}, where $\sqcup$ stands for the least upper bound (lub). Thus, a set can contain elements that can be assigned types, such that a lub can be computed for these types. Discussion on the computability of a lub for more complex terms is found in Buneman and Ohori [17].

Before describing the update operators and query language, we shall briefly introduce the notion of associative access. The dot operator is a common means for achieving this [50, 57], which is similar to field selection in Machiavelli [43]. For example, *Grad.advisor.Faculty.name* is an associative pattern which denotes the name of a faculty member who advises some graduate student. This dot expression could also have been written as *Grad.Faculty.name* since there is a unique path from *Grad* to *Faculty* via *advisor*. Also, the dot expression *joe.ss#* denotes the value 123123123 of type **integer**, and a set expression of the form { Student.name | ss# = 123123123 } denotes the singleton set, the element of which has the value "Joe" of type **string**.

The dot operator forms the basis of an associative pattern (or dot expression), and is directional. For example, let a and b be two classes, where a has an attribute s whose domain is b, and b has an attribute t whose domain is a. Thus, $a.b$ has a different denotation from $b.a$ since they result in values whose domains are different (assuming that there is a unique path from a to b and vice versa). Given such unique paths, s and t can be thought of as inverse attributes. The system does not automatically maintain inverse attributes. Therefore, even though a dot expression may be meaningful in one direction, it may not be defined in the reverse direction. It is possible for the user to specify the names of two classes as operands to the dot operator provided there exists an unambiguous path between the classes (or nodes in the schema graph). These dot expressions or associative patterns form an important component of the query sublanguage, as we shall see in the next chapter.

3.2 An Extensional Semantics for Classes

We shall now attempt to give an extensional semantics similar to that given in KANDOR [45]. In a Voltaire database, let $\mathcal{C}$ be the set of classes defined in it, let $\mathcal{A}$ be the set of attributes defined in it, $\mathcal{B}$ be the set of constraints (to model behavior), and let $\mathcal{I}$ be the set of instances defined in it. A partial model for a Voltaire database is then a set $\mathcal{D}$, the set of all instances, strings and numbers, plus a function $\mathcal{E}$ such that:

$$\mathcal{E} : \mathcal{C} \rightarrow 2^{\mathcal{D}}$$

This accounts for the fact that a given instance may belong to more than one class, due to multiple inheritance.

$$\mathcal{E} : \mathcal{A} \rightarrow (\mathcal{D} \rightarrow 2^{\mathcal{D}+})$$

where $\mathcal{D}+$ is the disjoint union of $\mathcal{D}$, numbers and strings. Thus, an attribute is treated as a function or two place predicate.

$\mathcal{E} : \mathcal{I} \rightarrow \mathcal{D}$

$\mathcal{E} : \mathcal{B} \rightarrow \mathcal{D}$

$\mathcal{E} : \textit{numerals} \rightarrow \textit{integers}$

$\mathcal{E} : \textit{realnumerals} \rightarrow \textit{real}$

$\mathcal{E} : \textit{strings} \rightarrow \textit{strings}$

The last three conditions account for base types supported by the system.

This function $\mathcal{E}$ effectively computes the extent of a given class. It may be thought of as being similar to a typical valuation function as found in denotational semantics. In order to compute the extent of a class, we must first compute the extent due to each syntactic category allowed in the definition of the class. Therefore, the various forms of $\mathcal{E}$ are defined above, and further, $\mathcal{E}$ must satisfy the following conditions:

1. $\mathcal{E}[a : c] = x$ where if $y = \mathcal{E}[a](x)$ then $y \in \mathcal{E}[c]$ and $x \in \mathcal{D}$

2. $\mathcal{E}[a : \textbf{set } c] = \{x \in \mathcal{D} \mid \text{ if } y \in \mathcal{E}[a](x) \text{ then } y \in \mathcal{E}[c]\}$

3. $\mathcal{E}[a : \textbf{tuple } a_i : c_i] = \prod_{i=1}^{n} \mathcal{E}[a.a_i : c_i]$

4. $\mathcal{E}[c : \textbf{constraint } b_1; \ldots; b_m] = \bigcap_{i=1}^{m} \mathcal{E}[c : \textbf{constraint } b_i]$

5. $\mathcal{E}[c : \textbf{constraint } b_i] = x$ if x satisfies the constraint b_i else $\emptyset$

6. $\mathcal{E}[c] = \bigcap_{i=1}^{n} \mathcal{E}[c_i] \cap \bigcap_{i=1}^{m} \mathcal{E}[a_i]$

   where the class c has superclasses $c_1 \ldots c_n$ and has attributes (with domain restrictions) $a_1 \ldots a_m$.

This type of model is called a partial model because it does not take into account the definitions of instances. The reason for this is that the definitions of instances are not important for determining the subclass relationship, because it does not depend on a particular model but on the entire set of models. Thus, c_1 is a subclass of c_2, i.e.,

$c_1 \preceq c_2$ *iff* $\mathcal{E}[c_1] \subseteq \mathcal{E}[c_2]$. It should be clear that a traditional characterization for this simple type discipline would ensure that the subclass relationship as defined above is decidable (provided that constraints are ignored). In fact, the formulation would be very similar to that of O_2, and is given in section 3.4. The above formulation is trivial since it does not yet account for functions, which we shall see in chapter 6.

The main reason for choosing the above semantics was to emphasize the extension of a given class. Our model makes no arbitrary assumptions. For example, the arity of an instance can be greater than that of the class(es) to which may it may belong. Also, multiple inheritance is possible without any problems. Instances are characterized by a unique identifier, the set of classes to which the instance may belong, and the set of attribute value pairs. An instance may belong to one or more classes provided it satisfies all constraints attached to a given class. The unique identifier is assigned to an instance by system (which also ensures its uniqueness across the system) at the time when the instance is created.

3.3 Update Operators

We also provide a set of update operators to create and modify existing instances. The **new** operator allows us to create a new persistent instance with an immutable, unique identifier as follows:

```
{ new.Student | ss# = 456456456 and name = "Smith" and
                major = { Dept | name = "EE" } and
                sections = { Section | sec_number = 8814 or
                                       sec_number = 7835 or
                                       sec_number = 8845 } }
```

This returns a unique identifier for a new instance of class *Student* which will now be stored in the database. The right hand side of the vertical bar "|" defines the values for each attribute of the instance. Assuming that there exists an instance defining the "EE" department, the value for *major* is given by the set expression

{Dept | name = "EE"}, which denotes the identifier *EE*. The value of ***gpa*** is not specified because there may be a constraint or rule which tells the system how to compute its value, i.e., ***gpa*** may be a derived attribute. Thus, before the instance is actually placed in the persistent store, the value for ***gpa*** would be computed and checked for consistency, but would not be made persistent along with the other values specified in the command.

The **modify** operator is like destructive assignment, in the sense that it will destroy a persistent value (other than the unique identifier), and replace it with a new value specified by the user. The modified instance is then checked for consistency before it is committed to the persistent store. This check is limited only to those classes to which the instance may belong. For example, { **modify**.joe | major = { Dept | name = "CS" } } changes the value of the *major* attribute of the object referenced by *joe*. Similarly, { **modify**.Person | age = **prev**.age + 1 } will increase the age of every instance of class *person* by 1. The **delete** operator actually destroys the (set of) instances specified by the user, e.g., { **delete**.Student | gpa < 1.0 }. These operators are also defined for non-persistent data values.[2]

3.4 On the Computability of Subclass

3.4.1 Object Graphs and Equality

Suppose we are given:

1. A finite set of *domains* $D_1, \ldots, D_n$, $n \geq 1$.

   Let $\mathcal{D}$ denote the union of all domains D_i.

2. A countably infinite set $\mathcal{A}$ of *attribute* names.

3. A countably infinite set $\mathcal{ID}$ of *identifiers.*

[2]The reason why **new, modify, delete** are defined for non-persistent values as well is that *persistence is a property of the instance* and not the class or type.

We now define the notion of *value.*

<u>*Definition 3.4.1.1*</u> *Values:*

1. The special symbol *null* is a value, called a *basic value.*

2. Every element v of $\mathcal{D}$ is a value, called a *basic value.*

3. Every finite subset of $\mathcal{ID}$ is a value, called a *set value.* Set values are denoted in the usual way using brackets.

4. The finite partial function $\tau : \mathcal{A} \rightarrow \mathcal{ID}$, denoted by $\langle a_1 : i_1, \ldots, a_p : i_p \rangle$, is defined on $a_1, \ldots, a_p$ such that $\tau(a_k) = i_k$ for all k from 1 to p. Every τ is called a *tuple value*

We denote by $\mathcal{V}$ the set of all values. We now define the notion of an object.

<u>*Definition 3.4.1.2*</u> *Objects:*

1. The set of all objects $\mathcal{O} = \mathcal{ID} \times \mathcal{V}$

2. An *object* is a pair $o = (i, v)$, where i is an element of $\mathcal{ID}$ (an identifier) and v is a value.

In $o = (i, v)$, if v is a basic value, then o is a basic object. Similarly, we can define *set-structured* and *tuple-structured* objects. Further, we define the functions $\iota : \mathcal{O} \rightarrow \mathcal{ID}$ and $\nu : \mathcal{O} \rightarrow \mathcal{V}$ such that $\iota(o)$ denotes the identifier i and $\nu(o)$ denotes the value of object o, respectively. We also define the function $\rho : \mathcal{O} \rightarrow 2^{\mathcal{ID}}$, which associates with an object the set of all identifiers appearing in its value, i.e., those referenced by the object. We can now define an Object Graph.

<u>*Definition 3.4.1.3*</u> *Object Graph:* Let Θ be a set of objects. Then, graph(Θ) is defined as follows:

---

1. If o is a basic object of Θ, then the graph contains a corresponding vertex with no outgoing edge. The vertex is labeled with the value of o, i.e., $\nu(o)$.

2. If o is the tuple-structured object $(i, \langle a_1 : i_1, \ldots, a_p, : i_p\rangle)$, then the subgraph in graph(Θ) corresponding to o contains a node (say, $\eta\bullet$) labeled with i, and p outgoing edges from η labeled with $a_1, \ldots, a_p$ leading respectively to nodes corresponding to objects $o_1, \ldots, o_p$ where each o_k is identified by i_k (provided such objects exist).

3. If o is a set-structured object $(i, \{i_1, \ldots, i_p\})$, then the graph of o consists of a node (say, $\eta*$) labeled by i, and p unlabeled outgoing edges from $\eta*$ leading respectively to nodes corresponding to objects $o_1, \ldots, o_p$ where each o_k is identified by i_k (provided such objects exist).

As an example, consider $\Theta = \{o_1, o_2, o_3, o_4, o_6, o_7, o_8\}$, where

$$o_1 = (i_1, \langle \text{name} : i_3, \text{dept} : i_4, \text{advisor} : i_2\rangle)$$

$$o_2 = (i_2, \langle \text{name} : i_6, \text{dept} : i_5, \text{address} : i_7, \text{advises} : i_1\rangle)$$

$$o_3 = (i_3, \text{“Jim”}),\ o_6 = (i_6, \text{“Joe”})\ o_4 = (i_4, \text{“CS”}),\ o_8 = (i_8, \text{“EE”})$$

$$o_5 = (i_5, \{i_4, i_8\})$$

$$o_7 = (i_7, \langle \text{city} : \mathit{null}, \text{zip} : \mathit{null}\rangle)$$

The objects o_1, o_2 and o_7 are tuple-structured, o_3, o_4, o_6 and o_8 are basic, and o_5 is set-structured. Θ is a consistent set of objects if it satisfies the definition given below.

<u>*Definition 3.4.1.4*</u> *Consistency of* Θ*:* A set Θ of objects is consistent iff

1. Θ is finite; and

2. the function ι is injective on Θ, i.e., there exist no pair of two objects with the same identifiers; and

3. $\forall\, o \in \Theta,\ \rho(o) \subseteq \iota(\Theta)$, i.e., every referenced identifier corresponds to an object Θ.

Definition 3.4.1.5 *Equality:*

1. 0-equality: two objects o and o' are 0-equal (or identical) iff $o = o'$

2. 1-equality: two objects o and o' are 1-equal iff $\nu(o) = \nu(o')$.

3. σ-equality: two objects o and o' are σ-equal iff span_tree(o) = span_tree(o' where span_tree(o) is the tree obtained from o by recursively replacing an identifier i (in a value) by the value of the object identified by i.

3.4.2 Classes, Types and Schemas

Definition 3.4.2.1 *Basic Class Names:*

Bnames is the set of names for basic classes containing:

1. The special symbols *Any* and *Nil.*

2. A symbol d_i for each domain $\mathcal{D}_i$. We denote $\mathcal{D}_i = dom(d_i)$.

3. A symbol $'x$ for every value x of $\mathcal{D}$.

Cnames is the set of names for constructed classes which is countably infinite and is disjoint with *Bnames.* This is because *Bnames* denotes the set of the names for basic domains such as boolean, string or integer. *Tnames* is the union of *Bnames* and *Cnames*, and it is the set of all names for classes.

In order to define classes, we assume there is a finite set $\mathcal{B}$ whose elements are constraints which describe the behavior of classes. For now, we shall consider elements of $\mathcal{B}$ as uninterpreted symbols.

Definition 3.4.2.2 Classes: A basic class is a pair (n,b), where n is an element of *Bnames* and b is a subset of $\mathcal{B}$.

A constructed class is one of the following:

1. A triple (s, t, b) where s is an element of *Cnames*, t is an element of *Tnames*, and b is a subset of $\mathcal{B}$. Such a class is denoted by $(s = t, b)$.

2. A triple (s, τ, b) where $s \in$ *Cnames*, and τ is a finite partial function $\tau : \mathcal{A} \rightarrow$ *Tnames*. Such a class is denoted by $s = \langle a_1 : s_1, \ldots, a_n : s_n \rangle, b)$, where $\tau(a_k) = s_k$, and is called a tuple-structured class.

3. A triple (s, s', b) where $s \in$ *Cnames*, $s' \in$ *Tnames*. Such a class is denoted by $(s = s', b)$ and is called a set-structured class.

A class is either basic or constructed, and the set of all classes is denoted by $\mathcal{T}$.

Definition 3.4.2.3 Class Structures

1. Basic Class Structure: Let $t = (n, m)$ be a basic class. Then n is called the basic class structure associated with t.

2. Constructed Class Structure: Let $t = (s = x, b)$ be a constructed class. Then $s = x$ is called the constructed type structure associated with t.

Given a class t, its structure is denoted by $\sigma(t)$ and its behavior by $\beta(t)$. We first give some notation before defining the notion of consistency for class structures.

1. If t is a class, then $\eta(t)$ denotes the name of the class.

2. if $\sigma(t)$ is a class structure associated with the class t, then we denote $\eta(\sigma(t)) = \eta(t)$.

3. If $\sigma(t)$ is a class structure associated with the class t, then we denote the set of all class names appearing in the structure of t (namely, $\sigma(t)$) by $refer(\sigma(t))$.

Definition 3.4.2.4 *Schemas:* A set Δ of constructed class structures is a *schema* if and only if:

1. Δ is a finite set; and

2. η is *injective* on Δ (i.e, there exists only one class structure for a given class name); and

3. $\forall \sigma(t) \in \Delta, refer(\sigma(t)) \cap Cnames \subseteq \eta(\Delta)$, i.e., there are no dangling identifiers.

The semantics of the class structure system defined above is given by a function which associates subsets of a consistent set of objects to class structure names.

Definition 3.4.2.5 *Interpretations:* Let Δ be a schema and Θ be a consistent subset of the universe of objects $\mathcal{O}$. An *interpretation* $\mathcal{I}$ of Δ in Θ is a function from *Tnames* to $2^{\iota(\Theta)}$, such that the following properties are satisfied.

A. Basic Class names

(a) $\mathcal{I}(Nil) \subseteq \{i \in \iota(\Theta) \mid (i, null) \in \Theta\}$.

The interpretation of *Nil* is a subset of the identifiers in Θ such that they denote objects whose value is *null.*

(b) $\mathcal{I}(d_i) \subseteq \{i \in \iota(\Theta) \mid \Theta(i) \in D_i\} \cup \mathcal{I}(\text{Nil})$.

The interpretation of a basic domain or type is the subset of identifiers of objects in Θ such that they denote basic objects in Θ.

(c) $\mathcal{I}('x) \subseteq \{i \in \iota(\Theta) \mid \Theta(i) = x\} \cup \mathcal{I}(\text{Nil})$.

(d) $\mathcal{I}(Any) = \{i \mid i \in \iota(\Theta)\}$.

Since all objects belong to *Any*, its interpretation is the set of all identifiers defined in Θ.

B. Constructed Class Names

(a) If $s = \langle a_1 : s_1, \ldots, a_n : s_n \rangle \in \Delta$, then $\mathcal{I}(s) \subseteq \{i \in \iota(\Theta) \mid \Theta(i)$ is a tuple-structured value defined at least on $a_1, \ldots, a_n$ and $\forall k\ \Theta(i)(a_k) \in \mathcal{I}(s_k)\} \cup \mathcal{I}(Nil)$.

(b) if $s = \{s'\} \in \Delta$, *then* $\mathcal{I}(s) \subseteq \{i \in \iota(\Theta) \mid \Theta(i) \subseteq \mathcal{I}(s')\} \cup \mathcal{I}(Nil)$.

(c) $(s = t) \in \Delta$, *then* $\mathcal{I}(s) \subseteq \mathcal{I}(t)$.

C. Undefined Class names

(a) If s is neither a class name nor the name of the schema Δ, then $\mathcal{I}(s) \subseteq \mathcal{I}(\text{Nil})$.

Definition 3.4.2.6 Model of a Schema

1. Partial order on Interpretations: An interpretation $\mathcal{I} \sqsubseteq \mathcal{I}'$ if and only if for all $s \in$ Tnames, $\mathcal{I}(s) \subseteq \mathcal{I}'(s)$.

2. Model: Let Δ be a schema and Θ be a consistent set of objects. The model $\mathcal{M}$ of Δ is Θ, which is the greatest interpretation of Δ in Θ.

Theorem 3.4.1 The definition of a Model is sound.

Proof of Theorem 3.4.1 Given a schema Δ and a consistent set of objects Θ, there are a finite number of interpretations of Δ defined on Θ. Therefore, in order to prove that the greatest interpretation exists, we have to prove that the union of two interpretations is an interpretation.

Let $\mathcal{I}_1$ and $\mathcal{I}_2$ be two interpretations and $\mathcal{I}(s) = \mathcal{I}_1(s) \cup \mathcal{I}_2(s)$, for every class name s. Clearly, $\mathcal{I}$ satisfies properties A.1, 2 and 3 of the definition above. Let $s = \langle a_1 : s_1, \ldots, a_n : s_n \rangle$, and i be an element of $\mathcal{I}(s)$. Then, i is either an element of $\mathcal{I}_1$ or $\mathcal{I}_2$. If i is an element of $\mathcal{I}_1$, then $\Theta(i)(a_k) \in \mathcal{I}(s_k)$ for all k, and $\mathcal{I}$ satisfies property B.1 above. Similarly, it can be shown that $\mathcal{I}$ satisfies properties B.2 and B.3 above. Thus, there exists a greatest interpretation $\mathcal{M}$ such that

$$\mathcal{M}(s) = \bigcup_{\mathcal{I} \in INT(\Delta)} \mathcal{I}(s),$$

for every class name s, where INT(Δ) denotes the set of all interpretations of Δ in Θ. ∎

Definition 3.4.2.7 Partial Order $\preceq$*:* Let s and s' be two class structures of a schema Δ. Then s is a substructure of s' (denoted by $s \preceq s'$) if and only if $\mathcal{M}(s) \subseteq \mathcal{M}(s')$ for all consistent sets Θ.

Theorem 3.4.2 If s and s' are two class structures of a schema Δ, then by $s \preceq s'$ if and only if one of the following conditions holds true:

1. s and s' are tuple structures $s = t$ and $s' = t'$, such that t is more defined than t' and for every attribute a such that t' is defined, $t(a) \preceq t'(a)$ holds.

2. s and s' are set structures such that $s = \{t\}$ and $s' = \{t'\}$, then $t \preceq t'$ holds.

3. $s = {}'x$, and s' is a basic class structure, and $x \in dom(s')$.

Proof of Theorem 3.4.2 The validity of this characterization can be established by induction. Completeness can be established on a case-by-case basis for tuple, set and basic class structures. ∎

This theorem provides a syntactical means for computing the subclass relationship, since we are ignoring the behavior of classes in this characterization.

Definition 3.4.2.8 ***Databases*** A database is a tuple $\langle \Delta, \Theta, \preceq, \mathcal{I} \rangle$ where

1. Δ is a consistent schema.
2. Θ is a consistent set of objects.
3. $\preceq$ is a partial order among elements of Δ.
4. $\mathcal{I}$ is an interpretation of Δ in Θ.

Further, the following properties must hold:

1. If $t \preceq t'$ and $t \preceq t''$, then $\sqcup\{t', t''\}$ is computable, provided $t' \neq$ Any and $t'' \neq$ Any. Further, t' and t'' are now said to be comparable, and $\sqcup\{t', t''\}$ is the least upper bound of t' and t''.
2. $\Theta = \bigcup_{t \in \Delta} \mathcal{I}(t)$

3.4.3 Glossary

Here we provide a brief glossary of some of the functions used in this section.

ι denotes the identifier of an object o

ν denotes the value of an object o

ρ associates with an object the set of all identifiers appearing in its value

τ is a partial function for tuple values

η denotes the name of a class

σ denotes the structure of a class

CHAPTER 4
QUERY SPECIFICATION

As mentioned earlier, Voltaire is an imperative programming language based on the notion of objects. Since query languages have traditionally been declarative and set-oriented, embedding them within a procedural, record-oriented framework inevitably leads to design conflicts. However, we avoid much of this conflict since Voltaire is a set-oriented language. This means that expressions, which form the core of Voltaire, denote a set of objects by default. For example, even the simple dot expression *Student.advisor.Faculty.dept* denotes a set of instances or objects whose type is the type of the attribute *dept*, such that each object participates in the association described in the dot expression. These same set expressions are used in specifying constraints in a class or function definition, with one important restriction. An expression of the form $s := \{c_1.[\ldots a_{1i} \ldots].c_2[\ldots a_{2j} \ldots]\ldots\}$ is not allowed even though it is well-typed: $type(s) = \{\langle \ldots, type(a_{1i}), \ldots, type(a_{2j}), \ldots \rangle\}$. The value of s would be a set of tuples, and each element in a tuple can contain nested sets and tuples. If such expressions were allowed, the run-time overhead would be very expensive.

Multiple inheritance does not create a problem when evaluating a query or set expression. This is because an instance can occur only within a unique context in the expression. The context is decided by the anchor class of the dot expression, which is simply the first class appearing in a dot expression. For example, in {TA.advisor | TA **in** RA}, the context is defined by the LHS of the "|", and therefore, the anchor class is *TA*. This query denotes the set of objects belonging to *type(advisor)* such that all instances of the class *TA* that have advisors are also members of the class *RA*. Even though the classes *TA* and *RA* are not subclasses of each other, they have common elements. Since the boolean condition *TA* **in** *RA* means **self in** *RA* (where **self** maintains currency in the set of objects belonging to the anchor class), the query can be evaluated without conflict.

4.1 The Basic Structure of a Query

The basic structure of the query sublanguage is as shown below:

<set_expr> ::= { <E> '|' <Bool> } | { <E> } | <E> | <agg_op> <set_expr>

<Bool> ::= (<Bool>) | **not** <Bool> | < Bool$_1$ > **or** < Bool$_2$ > |
< Bool$_1$ > **and** < Bool$_2$ > | < E$_1$ > <rel-op> < E$_2$ > |
< E$_1$ > = < E$_2$ > | **forall** <E> : <Bool> |
exists <E> | **dbexists** <E>

<E> ::= <dot_expr> | − <term> | <term> | <term> <add-op> <E>

The query sublanguage consists of associative set expressions. The user specifies a path (or subgraph) of interest on the LHS of the vertical bar, and simple boolean predicates for selection conditions on the RHS of the vertical bar. This path of interest denotes the context of the set expression within which certain boolean conditions must hold true. The context is also important since it defines the scope of identifiers (this will be further elaborated in section 6.6). A simple context can be specified by using a dot expression. An important restriction is that the first identifier in a dot expression on the LHS which defines the context must be a class name. This class is then called the *anchor* class. The syntactic category <E> denotes expressions which are simple extensions to those found in most languages such as Pascal. To project attributes of a class referenced in the dot expression, they are enclosed within square brackets. We show a few examples (some taken from Alashqur et al [2]) below with respect to the schema graph depicted in figure 2.

4.2 Examples

Q 1. Project the names of all graduate students who teach other graduate students in some sections. Also, project the names of those graduate students they teach.

{ TA[name].teaches.Section.Grad[name] }

Note that the class *TA* inherits two attributes whose domain is the class *Section*, namely, *teaches* from the class *Teacher* and *sections* from the class *Grad* (via *Student*). Since we are interested in *TA*s in their role as *Teachers* (and not as graduate students who also enroll in course sections), we appropriately include *teaches* in the dot expression.

Q 2. Project the names of all departments that offer 6000 level courses that have a current offering (i.e., sections). Also, project the titles of these courses and the textbook used in each section.

$$\{ \text{Dept[name].Course[title].Section[textbook]} \mid \text{Course.c\#} \leq 6000 \ \textbf{and} \ \text{Course.c\#} < 7000 \}$$

A department offers many courses, i.e., the class *Dept* has an attribute *course_offering* whose domain is the class *Course*. Similarly, each *Course* may have one or more *Sections*. This query is evaluated by first accessing all instances of the class *Dept*. For each instance of *Dept*, we retrieve the object references to all courses offered by that *Dept*. These instances of class *Course* are then filtered through the boolean conditions to check if the corresponding course numbers lie between 6000 and 7000. All instances of *Course* which do not satisfy this condition are dropped from further consideration. For each instance of *Course* so far selected, we access the corresponding *Sections* for that course.

Q 3. Project the names of all graduate students who are *RA*s but not *TA*s.

{ RA.name | **not** (RA **in** TA) }

The boolean condition could have also been specified as **not** (**self in** TA). This is because any dot expression on the RHS of the vertical bar beginning with the anchor class means the same as **self**. **Self** is a special operator used to define currency in a set processing stream.

Q 4. Project the names of all under-graduate students whose minor is in that department which is the the major department of the under-graduate student with ss# = 123456789.

{Undergrad.name | Undergrad.minor.Dept =

{Undergrad.major.Dept | Undergrad.ss# = 123456789}}

The boolean condition in this query has an embedded set expression. The scope of a dot expression (i.e., context) is local to the set expression in which it occurs. Therefore, in the inner set expression, we are interested in the major department of that instance of class *Undergrad* whose ss# has the value 123456789. Similarly, in the outer set expression, we are interested in that *Undergrad* whose minor *Dept* has the same value as that specified by the embedded set expression. In order to transcend the scope of a dot expression from an inner to outer set expression (or vice versa), we must use special operators such as **prev**, and will be seen in chapter 6.

Q 5. Project the names of all TAs who grade courses in which they themselves are registered (i.e., enrolled).

{ TA.name | **self**.teaches.Section **in** **self**.enrolled.Section }

We are interested in those instances of *TA* that teach some section of a course in which that same instance of *TA* is enrolled. Since a *TA* may be taking more than one course, but can teach only one course, we use the set inclusion operator. Again, **self** could have been replaced by *TA*.

Q 6. What would be the values for salary for all research assistants whose advisor is Smith, if they were to receive a 20% increment?

$$\{\ 1.2 \times (\text{RA.salary}) \mid \text{RA.advisor.Faculty.name} = \text{“Smith”}\ \}$$

This query would first evaluate the set expression and then multiply each projected value of salary by the scalar 1.2. If the context were to have more than one subexpression containing the dot operator, then the first dot expression from the left would be chosen as the context, and the remaining ones would be interpreted as if they were on the RHS of the vertical bar.

4.3 Aggregate Operators

Several aggregate operators such as **count, sum, min, max** are provided. These are not really special operators, but are mainly provided for convenience. These can be easily defined by using a homomorphic set extension operator [17].

$$\begin{aligned}\textbf{let hom} \;&=\; \lambda(f, op, z, S).S = \{\} \rightarrow z| \\ &\quad\ \textbf{tail}\ S = \{\} \rightarrow op(f(\textbf{head}\ S), z)| \\ &\quad\ op(f(\textbf{head}\ S), \textbf{hom}(f, op, z, \textbf{tail}\ S))\end{aligned}$$

There is an alternative form of this function that applies to non-empty sets, and does not require the argument z.

$$\textbf{let hom}^* \;=\; \lambda(f, op, S).op(f(\textbf{head}\ S), \textbf{hom}{*}(f, op, \textbf{tail}\ S))$$

Thus, we can now define the following:

$\textbf{let sum} = \lambda S.\textbf{hom}(\lambda x.x, +, 0, S)$

let count $= \lambda S.\mathbf{hom}(\lambda x.1, +, 0, S)$

let min $= \lambda S.\mathbf{hom*}(\lambda x.x, \lambda(x,y).x < y \rightarrow x|y, S)$

This above formulation gives us a way to define and compute these aggregation operators for sets of arbitrary structures, and are guaranteed of getting a correct result that is free of side-effects.

4.4 Evaluation Strategies

4.4.1 Semantics of the Dot Operator

Set theoretic definition. Let C_1, C_2 be class names, $\mathcal{E}[C_1], \mathcal{E}[C_2]$ be the extents of C_1, C_2 and $c_{1_i}, c_{2_j} \in \mathcal{E}[C_1], \mathcal{E}[C_2]$ respectively. Let C_1 have an attribute labeled a_{1_k}, whose domain is C_2. Effectively, given a schema graph with two nodes C_1, C_2, there must exist a unique path from C_1 to C_2 for $C_1.C_2$ to be meaningful. Let $\mathcal{S}$ denote the aggregation association from C_1 to C_2 via the attribute a_{1_k} such that $\mathcal{S} \subseteq \mathcal{E}[C_1] \times \mathcal{E}[C_2]$, where a_{1_k} is an attribute of C_1. Thus,

$$C_1.C_2 = \{c_{2_j} \mid c_{1_i} \in \mathcal{E}[C_1] \wedge c_{2_j} \in \mathcal{E}[C_2] \wedge (c_{1_i}, c_{2_j}) \in \mathcal{S}\}$$

If the domain of a_{1_k} is **set** C_2, then $\mathcal{S} \subseteq \mathcal{E}[C_1] \times 2^{\mathcal{E}[C_2]}$ and let $C_{2_j} \subseteq \mathcal{E}[C_2]$. Then,

$$C_1.C_2 = \{c_{2_j} \mid c_{1_i} \in \mathcal{E}[C_1] \wedge c_{2_j} \in C_{2_j} \wedge (c_{1_i}, C_{2_j}) \in \mathcal{S}\}$$

In general, let $C_1, \ldots, C_n$ denote class names and $\mathcal{E}[C_1], \ldots, \mathcal{E}[C_n]$ denote their respective extents. Let c_{i_k} be the kth element of $\mathcal{E}[C_i]$. Let $\mathcal{S}_i$ be a meaningful aggregation association (in the sense mentioned above) between C_i and C_{i+1}, such that $\mathcal{S}_i \subseteq \mathcal{E}[C_i] \times \mathcal{E}[C_{i+1}]$ (or, if the domain that unique attribute a_{i_k} of C_i is **set** C_{i+1}, then $\mathcal{S}_i \subseteq \mathcal{E}[C_i] \times 2^{\mathcal{E}[C_{i+1}]}$). Also, $C_0.C_1 \equiv \mathcal{E}[C_1]$. Then,

$$C_1.\cdots.C_{n-1}.C_n = \{c_{n_k} \mid c_{n_k} \in \mathcal{E}[C_n] \wedge c_{n-1_j} \in C_1.\cdots.C_{n-2}.C_{n-1} \wedge (c_{n-1_j}, c_{n_k}) \in \mathcal{S}_{n-1}\}$$

Model theoretic definition. We now give a formal definition of the dot operator with respect to the algebra defined in section 3.4. Let $C_i \in \mathcal{T}$, where $\mathcal{T}$ is the set of all types in the schema. Then $\eta(C_i) \in \eta(\mathcal{T})$ where η is the name function. Let $c_{i_j} \in \mathcal{I}(C_i)$ where $\mathcal{I}(C_i)$ is the interpretation of C_i. Then $\eta(C_i).\eta(C_{i+1})$ is valid if and only if $\sigma(\eta(C_i)) = \langle a_{i_1} : s_{i_1} \dots a_{i_n} : s_{i_n} \rangle \wedge \exists a_{n_k} : \tau(a_{n_k}) = s_{n_k} \wedge \mathcal{I}(s_{n_k}) \subseteq \mathcal{I}(C_{i+1})$. Clearly, then $\eta(C_i).\eta(C_{i+1}) \subseteq \mathcal{I}(C_{i+1})$. Recall that $\sigma(C_i)$ denotes the structure of C_i, and τ is the partial function defined on tuple structures. For brevity, we drop η, so that $C_i.C_{i+1}$ means the same as $\eta(C_i).\eta(C_{i+1})$, and also $C_0.C_1 \equiv \mathcal{I}(C_1)$. Now,

$$C_1.\cdots C_{n-1}.C_n = \{c_{n_j} \mid c_{n_j} \in \mathcal{I}(C_n) \wedge \exists a_{n_k} : \tau(a_{n_k})(c_{n_j}) \in C_{n-2}.C_{n-1}\}.$$

4.4.2 Naive Approach

As we have seen, queries are formulated in an associative fashion via the dot operator. The LHS of a set expression defines the context in which the boolean conditions on the RHS are to be evaluated. These boolean conditions are also formulated with the dot operator. Therefore, it seems reasonable to investigate the semantics of the dot operator, and a means to evaluate it. We first give a simple example, and an obvious operational meaning for a set expression. Let A, B, C, D, E, F, G, H be class names. The dot operator is said to be meaningful for $A.B$ if and only if there exists an attribute in A whose domain is B or a subtype of B (as was formalized above). Now consider the query:

$$\{A.B.C.D.E \mid C.G = E.H\} \equiv \{A.B.C.D.E \mid A.B.C.G = A.B.C.D.E.H\}$$

This query can be evaluated as follows:

```
result := null;
for each a ∈ A
   for each b ∈ B
      for each c ∈ C
         for each d ∈ D
            for each e ∈ E
               for each h ∈ H
```

```
if (((a.b).c).g) = ((((a.b).c).d).e).h then
   result := union(result, e);
```

Note that $(a.b)$ is similar to the usual record selection operator except for the implicit assumption that there exists an attribute in class A whose type is B. The parentheses define the order of evaluation. For example, if the current object in A is o_A, and A_k is the attribute label in question, then $a.b = \tau(o_A)(A_k)$, where τ is the usual record selection function.

However, as mentioned earlier, the only way to override the scope of an identifier within a set expression (and, therefore, a context) is to use **prev**. For example, consider the following:

$$\{A.B.C.D.E \mid C.G = \mathbf{prev}.E.H\} \equiv \{A.B.C.D.E \mid A.B.C.G = E.H\}$$

This query can be evaluated as follows:

```
result := null;
for each a ∈ A
   for each b ∈ B
      for each c ∈ C
         for each d ∈ D
               for each e ∈ E
                  for each h ∈ H
                     if (((a.b).c).g) = e.h then
                        result := union(result, e);
```

4.4.3 Algebraic Approach

As we have seen, the query language essentially consists of dot expressions, which form the context on the LHS and selection conditions on the RHS of the vertical bar. However, it is possible to evaluate these queries using extended algebraic operators [50, 53, 56]. Thus, the compiler can exploit existing query optimization techniques. For example, the first example can be transformed by the compiler to the following form[1]:

[1] The actual definitions in Shaw and Zdonick [50] are slightly different, but we are using a simpler notation for sake of clarity.

$T_1 = \bowtie_{\theta_1} (Section,\ Grad)$ where

$\theta_1 \equiv\ Grad$ **in** $Section.enrollment$

$T_2 = \pi_{Section.oid,\ Grad.name}(T_1)$

$T_3 = \bowtie_{\theta_2} (TA, T_2)$ where

$\theta_2 \equiv TA.teaches$ **in** $T_2.Section.oid$

$T_4 = \pi_{TA.name,\ Grad.name}(T_3)$

Similarly, { (RA.salary) | RA.advisor.Faculty.name = "Smith" }, can be transformed to:

$\pi_{salary}(\sigma_{\theta}(RA))$, where

$\theta \equiv RA.advisor = \pi_{oid}(\sigma_{name="Smith"}(Faculty))$

An algebraic formulation can also be used to define a dataflow implementation of the query processor. Since Voltaire expressions are set-oriented, a parallel implementation is possible:

{<Dot_expr> | < Bool_1 > **and** < Bool_2 >} ≡

{<Dot_expr> | < Bool_1 >} ∩ {<Dot_expr> | < Bool_2 >}

{<Dot_expr> | < Bool_1 > **or** < Bool_2 >} ≡

{<Dot_expr> | < Bool_1 >} ∪ {<Dot_expr> | < Bool_2 >}

In general, it is possible to show that the dot operator and boolean conditions can be reduced to a small set of algebraic operators as described in the literature [50, 53, 56].

CHAPTER 5
CONSTRAINT SPECIFICATION

Automatic integrity enforcement is a non-trivial problem [13, 21, 39, 40, 46, 55]. For example, when the consequent of a rule results in a database update operation, detecting possible infinite regression due to update propagation simply adds to the complexity. Another problem is that of maintaining cross-references. For example, suppose a rule states that every graduate must have an advisor. If a certain faculty member who advises three graduate students leaves the university, and is therefore deleted from the database, then these three instances of graduate students will be in an inconsistent state. Automatic update propagation may be dangerous since we certainly would not like to delete the three graduate students merely because their advisor left. A better way to deal with such situations is to introduce an elaborate exception handling mechanism. Thus, we can state an exception to the above rule such that the graduate students in question must find another advisor within three months from the time the faculty member was deleted. Exception handling and active database management are outside the scope of this dissertation.

There are two important characteristics about constraint management in Voltaire:

1. unlike most other constraint languages, the order in which constraints appear is significant (reasons for this will be clear only after chapter 6), and

2. since the execution model is lazy (as derived attributes are computed on demand only), and the effects of **modify** are only local, the user can never access inconsistent data in the persistent store.[1]

[1]This is precisely the view taken in Jagadish [31].

This is because an instance can belong to a given class if and only if it satisfies all the constraints specified in the definition of that class.[2] Lazy evaluation implies that constraints in Voltaire are automatically triggered whenever a new instance is created or an existing instance is modified.

5.1 Basic Structure of Constraints

The basic structure of constraints is as shown below:

<B> ::= < B_1 > ; < B_2 > | <Bool> | < Comm_1 >

< Comm_1 > ::= **if** <Bool> **then** <B> **endif** |
if <Bool> **then** < B_1 > **else** < B_2 > **endif**

<Bool> ::= ... | < E_1 >=< E_2 > | ...

It is important to note that the antecedent of a constraint is structurally and semantically identical to the selection (i.e., boolean) conditions, which form the RHS of the vertical bar in a set expression. The consequent of a constraint can also be a boolean condition, in which case satisfiability is computed. However, when the consequent contains the equality operator, two possibilities arise. If both the RHS and LHS are bound, then satisfiability is checked. If the LHS of the equality operator is unbound, then a binding takes place. That is, the equality operator is overloaded. Further, when a constraint does not have an antecedent (as in rules 1 and 2 in *Student* below), it behaves like an equational constraint which must be satisfied (in one direction only). We now look at a few examples.

5.2 Examples

5.2.1 Constraints on the class *Student*

1. Student.total_work = Student.total_credit + Student.job_hours

[2]This means that if a class can be found such that its constraints are satisfied by the instance in question, then the class of this instance can be automatically inferred.

2. Student.leisure_time = 80 − Student.total_work;

3. Student.leisure_time > 20;

4. **if** Student.visa_status = "F-1" **then** Student.job_hours ≤ 20;

Rule 2 specifies how to compute the leisure time of a student, whereas rule 3 places a bound on the possible values that a student's leisure time can have. When a new instance of class *Student* is created, the total work may not be known. Therefore, before the value of leisure time can be computed, rule 1 must be triggered. When the value for the total number of credit hours for which a student may be registered or job hours is modified, rules 1, 2, 3 and 4 are triggered. Rule 4 states that for all students whose visa status is F-1, they will not be allowed to work for more than 20 hours.

Since all of the above constraints are attached to the single class *Student* there is no need to repeat the class name. For example, rule 1 could be rewritten as ***total_work*** = ***total_credit*** + ***job_hours***, with an implicit **self** operator prepended to each attribute. The **self** operator keeps track of the specific instance in question at all times during the state of a computation.

Consider a program segment where a new instance of class *Grad* is created:

jim = { **new**.Grad | ss# = 123456789 **and** name = "jim brown"
and ... **and** total_credit = 12 **and** job_hours = 20 };

Before this instance can be placed in the persistent store, domain and other constraints must be checked. Since a new instance is being created, attributes occurring on the RHS of the vertical bar are bound to their corresponding values. Rules 1, 2, 3 and 4 are now triggered. The first two rules result in the computation of ***total_work*** and *leisure_time*. Rule 3 checks the condition *leisure_time* > 20 hours, which is satisfied in our example. Suppose that nothing is mentioned about *visa_status* when the instance is being created. If the domain constraints of that attribute allow a null value, then 4 is ignored, else an error condition is reported.

Suppose a modify command is issued where Jim's leisure time is updated to a new value. This would trigger rules 2 and 3. Rule 2 is an equational constraint on the relationship between *leisure_time*, *total_credit* and *job_hours*. Thus, if a new value for *leisure_time* does not satisfy 2, then an error condition is reported, even though 3 may be satisfied. Integrity enforcement in this situation is not possible due to the inherent nondeterminism. However, any update to *total_credit* or *job_hours* is propagated in the obvious way.

5.2.2 Constraints on the class *Grad*

1. **if exists** Grad.thesis_option **then**

   exists Grad.advisor **and** Grad.advisor **in** Grad.committee;

2. **for all** Grad.section.course.c# : c# ≥ 5000;

3. **if** Grad.status = "full-time" **then** Grad.total_credit ≥ 12;

4. **if** course_work = "done" **and** thesis_status = "defended" **and**

   count { committee.Faculty | Faculty.Dept **includes self** .Dept } ≥ 2

   then degree_req = "fulfilled";

In the consequent of Rule 1, we need an existential quantifier because if *Grad.advisor* evaluates to a null set, then it would be trivially contained in *Grad.committee*, which is not the intended semantics. Rule 2 states that all the course numbers taken by any graduate student must be of level 5000 or greater. Rule 3 states that all graduate students attending school full time must register for at least 12 credit hours.

5.3 Null Values and Exceptions

Information is often not always available when a new record or instance is being created. This means that there may be a number of attributes of the instance in question with null values. These instances are nevertheless useful since they contain at least partial information about some real world entity. Dealing with the issue of null values involves certain compromises since it conflicts with the following fact. Null values may violate the structural and/or behavioral constraints of the class (or type) to which the instance belongs. Thus, loading a database with null values may jeopardize the safeness in a type system, and the user may thereby encounter run-time errors. These errors could otherwise have been detected when the database was being loaded. We have chosen a compromise in which:

1. The value **null** can be coerced to belong to any type.[3] Thus, the structural constraints of a type need not be violated.

2. It is very likely that the behavioral constraints can be violated due to the presence of null values (i.e., the absence of information). But since we have adopted a lazy evaluation mode, derived attributes are not computed until actually requested. Thus, the user will not receive inconsistent instances as a part of the result of a query.

Another way that the user can deal with null values is by defining constraints with the help of the **exists** operator. Suppose that most graduate students must have advisors, though not all of them may have one (probably because the student

[3]Actually, the type of **null** is **Nil** , and **Nil** is always a subtype of any other type that is defined in the type scheme.

has not yet found a suitable advisor). Further, if the student does have an advisor, then the advisor must belong to the same department as the student. This constraint can be modeled as follows:

if exists Grad.advisor **then**
  Grad.dept = Grad.advisor.dept;

By defining this rule, an instance of the class *Grad* can have a null value in its *advisor* attribute, and at the same time not violate a *behavioral* constraint. Further, this can also be used as a means to deal with simple exceptions, thus avoiding a proliferation of subclasses such as *Grad_with_advisor* and *Grad_without_advisor* whose superclass is *Grad*. As another example, suppose that every graduate student must register for at least 12 credits, except Joe, who is allowed to register for any number of credits. This can be modeled as follows:

if Grad.name ≠ "Joe" **then**
  Grad.credit_hours ≥ 12;

Constraint specification is very similar to what is found in most other systems, except that the order in which the constraints appear is significant. We have shown that it is possible to bootstrap the constraint specification sublanguage on top of the query sublanguage. We also show how to exploit null values to deal with incomplete information and exceptions. Constraints in Voltaire get triggered whenever an instance is created or modified. Further, functions are computed as the result of integrity enforcement, as we shall see in the next chapter.

CHAPTER 6
FUNCTION SPECIFICATION

Traditionally, in the database world, a function or application is implemented in a host language with embedded DML statements. This application is then executed independently of the DBMS under the control of the operating system. Thus, the DBMS only knows of a transaction defined by a block of DML statements, and has no way of knowing whether an application as a whole will succeed or not. This may cause run-time aborts, which are expensive to handle. In contrast, the application is executed under the control of a central transaction manager within a DBPL, and the application is implemented as a function or method (in object-oriented database systems). However, the problem of defining a transaction is still an area of on-going research. In a DBPL, a function is expected to be compiled into a transaction sublanguage which gets executed each time a function is to be evaluated at a higher level. However, such issues are outside the scope of this dissertation. Here, we shall merely concern ourselves with the evaluation and semantics of function specification in Voltaire.

Functions in Voltaire rely heavily on the dot operator for associative access, and set expressions for computing denotable values. A function is specified as a sequence of constraints or commands, in a manner similar to the imperative paradigm. That is, each command is executed sequentially. Further, the user can write programs without worrying about using different operators for persistent and non-persistent objects. For example, the **new** operator creates a location for an instance of a given class, and returns a denotable value of domain *Ref.* Consider the expression:

$s := \{\mathbf{new}.c \mid \ldots a_i = v_i \ldots\}$. If s is not persistent within the context of evaluation, it is bound to a denotable value belonging to the domain *Ref*. On the other hand, if s is a persistent value within the context of evaluation, then it gets bound to a denotable value belonging to the domain *Ref* in the run-time environment, and also gets reflected in the persistent store. In either case, the symbol s provides a consistent handle to the value referenced by it in the run-time environment. Similarly, if the **modify** operator is applied to a non-persistent object, its effect is made available only to the run-time environment, whereas, if it applied to a persistent object, its effect is reflected in the persistent store (i.e., database) as well the run-time environment. We now examine the basic structure of a Voltaire function with the help of a simple factorial example, followed by a database example.

6.1 Basic Structure of a Function

Function specification can be thought of as a set of rules or constraints defining the relationship between its input and output parameters. Thus, by extending the constraint sublanguage to include a few additional constructs, we can write an arbitrary function in Voltaire.

< Comm_2 > ::= < Comm_1 > | <Assignment> | <Loop> |
<dml-ops> | <io>

<Assignment> ::= <dot_expr> := <set_expr>

<Loop> ::= <Iterator> | <While>
<Iterator> ::= **for each** <I> **in** <set_expr> **do** <B> **enddo**
<While> ::= **while** <Bool> **do** <B> **enddo**

<io> ::= <open> | <close> | <print> | <read>

Additionally, functions can have an extent which is persistent, or a function call (via dot expressions) may result in the non-persistent creation of instance(s) of that function for the duration of a computation. These temporary instances form the backbone of the execution model of a Voltaire program in which

1. functions and classes are treated uniformly, and

2. function evaluation is the result of integrity enforcement.

We first elaborate with the help of a simple example.

```
class Fact function
attributes
    n: integer
    f: integer
constraints
    if n = 0 then f = 1;
    if n > 0 then f = n × { Fact.f | Fact.n = prev.n − 1 };
```

The function *Fact* has two parameters, namely *n* and *f*; looked upon as a class, it has two (corresponding) attributes. The left hand side of the "|" operator defines the context within which the right hand side is evaluated. Thus, *n* refers to the attribute value of a new copy of *Fact*, and is bound to **prev**.$n - 1$ (where **prev**.n is bound to that value of n immediately outside the set expression). For example, we can obtain the factorial of 6 by issuing the following command: **eval** {Fact.f | Fact.n = 6} in the Voltaire environment. When the function is initially invoked, *n* is bound to the value 6, while *f* is unbound. The expression **prev**.*n* then refers to the value of *n* that is immediately outside the set expression, namely 6. Thus **prev**.$n - 1$ denotes the value 5. Also, the equality operator is overloaded such that when the LHS is initially unbound, it gets bound to the RHS value; when the LHS is initially bound, satisfiability is computed. The attribute *f* remains unbound until the recursion begins to unwind. Additionally, there is an implicit coercion on the set expression to an object of type integer due to the semantics of the × operator. Since one operand is an integer and the other is a set of integers (due to the set expression), coercion is necessary for the proper evaluation of the × operator.

It must be noted that the set expression can also be construed as a query. For example, the subexpression, {Fact.f | Fact.n = **prev**.n-1} also means "retrieve all objects of class *Fact* such that *Fact.n* is the same as *n-1* for some other instance of class *Fact*". Thus, if there were a database consisting of instances of class *Fact*, i.e., value pairs of *n* and *f*, then a query asking for the factorial of 6 could result in a simple look-up. Alternately, the same sub-expression can be interpreted as "compute the result of function *Fact* given the value of *n*" (i.e., function call). This is because classes and functions are treated uniformly in Voltaire.

Aggregate operators such as **sum** are provided as a convenience, but it is easy to write such a function in Voltaire as shown below:

```
class Sum function
attributes
    operand: list integer
    result: integer
constraints
    result = head.operand + {Sum.result | Sum.operand = tail.prev.operand}
```

While the above program is similar to the factorial function, it would have been more efficient to have written it as follows:

```
for each x in operand do
    { modify.Sum | result = prev.result + x }
enddo
```

6.2 A Database Example

In order to compare the expressive power of various DBPLs, a task list has been described in [5]. Here, we show how some of these tasks can be performed in Voltaire. The first task is to be able to describe a fragment of a manufacturing company's parts inventory. Among other things, the database represents the way certain parts are manufactured out of other parts: the subparts that are involved in the manufacture of other parts, the cost of manufacturing a part from its subparts, the mass increment that occurs when the subparts are assembled. The manufactured parts themselves may be subparts in a further manufacturing process, thus representing an aggregation hierarchy. In addition, the part name, its supplier and purchase cost is also maintained in the database. A partial Voltaire schema for this database is shown below.

```
class Part                      class Compositepart
superclasses Any                superclasses Part
subclasses                      subclasses nil
    Basepart Compositepart
attributes                      attributes
    name: string                    assemblycost: integer
    used_in: Compositepart          massincrement: integer
                                    uses: set Use

class Basepart                  class Use
superclasses Part               superclasses Any
subclasses nil                  subclasses nil
attributes                      attributes
    cost: integer                   component: Part
    mass: integer                   assembly: Compositepart
    supplied_by: Supplier           quantity: integer
```

The second task is to write a program to print the names, cost and mass of all base parts that cost more than 100 dollars. This can be achieved by writing a simple query, namely, { Basepart[name, cost, mass] | cost $\geq$ 100 }

The next task is to compute and print the total cost of a part as shown below. This task defeats most query languages because it requires the computation of transitive closure over the parts hierarchy in the database. To compute the cost of a pump,

---

we simply invoke the function as follows: { ComputeCost.resultcost | partname = "pump" }.

```
class ComputeCost function
attributes
    partname: string
    resultcost: integer
transients
    p: Part
    el_cost: integer
    subcosts: list integer
constraints

    p = { Part | name = partname };
    if p in Basepart then
        resultcost = p.cost
    else
        for each y in p.uses.component
        do
            el_cost := p.uses.quantity × { ComputeCost.resultcost |
                partname = y.partname } },
            { modify.subcosts | head.subcosts = el_cost and
                tail.subcosts = prev.subcosts }
        enddo;
        resultcost = p.assemblycost + { sum | subcosts }
    endif
```

The keyword **transients** denotes temporary attributes and has the same semantics as regular attributes, except that they are not persistent. Transient attributes do not reflect the final state of a computation, but merely facilitates a more efficient evaluation of a function. Therefore, they can be seen to behave like local variables. The first statement assigns the object identifier of that instance of *Part* referenced via its *name*, to the transient variable *p*. In the second statement, there is an iterator which has two commands. The first one makes a recursive call to the function to descend the aggregation hierarchy, and temporarily stores the cost of an element in *el_cost.* The second command needs more elaboration. As the recursion unfolds, the element costs are collected in the list *subcosts*. The effect of the **modify** operator is similar to *subcosts* := **append**(*el_cost, subcosts*). However, since *subcosts* is a temporary attribute, it merely refers to some object (here, a list of integers) in virtual memory. Therefore, the effects of **modify** will be limited only to virtual memory. On the other hand, if the RHS of the vertical bar referred to some persistent objects, then **modify** would appropriately make changes in the persistent store. Also, if we had used the function *Sum* defined in the previous section, then the last command in the *ComputeCost* function would have been written as:

resultcost = p.assemblycost + { Sum.result | operand = subcosts }

6.3 Temporary Instance Creation

Let us recapitulate some features of Voltaire. We began with the premise that certain database and programming capabilities must be incorporated within a uniform framework. We chose integrity enforcement as that unifying framework. The main reason why functions can also be computed is that the execution model treats the constraints as a sequence of statements to be evaluated in the order in which they appear. In fact, these expressions have a semantics in which new bindings are passed on to the next expression to be evaluated.[1] It is a direct consequence of this execution model that *classes* and *functions* can truly be equivalent.[2] This equivalence was important because we insisted that the query language be able to reference classes and make function calls with the *same* syntax and semantics. The inability of a query language to uniformly access classes and functions causes various paradigm mismatch problems [7, 12]. Typically, query languages allow function calls via ad

[1]We now see why the order in which constraints appeared in the classes *Grad* and *Student* was important.

[2]Manuel Bermudez suggested collectively calling them *clunctions*.

hoc trigger mechanisms, something we wish to avoid since it would create problems in defining and executing a transaction.

Now, consider the set expression:

{ Student.total_hours | ss# = 987654321 **and** name = "john" **and** ... };

When such a program segment is encountered, the evaluation function will first search for an instance existing in the database. If the search fails, it will then attempt to create a temporary instance which must satisfy all the constraints in the definition of class *Student*. Effectively, this failure is a function call. The semantics of such an expression can be construed to denote the value for *total_hours* of a hypothetical student that satisfies the bindings on the RHS of the "|" operator. This might be useful in a context where (in the ensuing program sequence) this temporary instance is to be made persistent if, say, *total_hours* evaluates to greater than 40:

x = { Student | ss# = 987654321 **and** name = "john" **and** ... };
if x.total_work $\geq$ 40 **then** { **new**.Student | x };

The first statement results in a binding. The identifier x is bound to a reference (unique identifier) to an instance of class *Student*. As mentioned earlier, if "john" does not exist in the database, then the set expression results in a function call, and x is bound to a reference to a temporary instance. This temporary instance must satisfy all constraints of class *Student*, and all derived attributes are also computed. If for this instance, the condition *total_work* $\geq$ 40 holds true, then this instance is made persistent by using the **new** operator. In this way a temporary instance can be made persistent. Thus, temporary instance creation forms the backbone of our execution model which allows us to give an equivalent semantics to classes and functions.

6.4 A Model of Inheritance for Classes and Functions

A problem with equivalence of classes and functions is that we now have to understand what the notion of subclass (or subfunction) means. The subclass relationship can be defined as follows. Let f, g be two classes and $\mathcal{E}[f]$ $\mathcal{E}[g]$ denote their respective extensions. Then f is said to be a subclass of g iff $\mathcal{E}[f] \subseteq \mathcal{E}[g]$. Such extensional semantics have been defined for term subsumption languages [45]. However, the subclass (or subsumption) relationship is computable by performing a structural analysis of the class taxonomy.[3] Such analysis is based on a set of inference rules for computing subsumption. For example, CANDIDE [11] is a carefully constrained language in which the subclass relationship (called subsumption) is decidable [11] [45] and its complexity is at least co-NP-hard [42]. But this is clearly an undecidable proposition in Voltaire because we allow arbitrary constraints to be specified in the class (and function) definition.

Our proposed solution is based on the realization that we are primarily interested in only those values that exist in the persistent store (i.e., database), as opposed to the possibly infinite set of instances that may belong to a given class.[4] Additionally, we are also interested in instances temporarily created within the context of some program. Note that a class can be viewed to have base attributes and derived attributes, while in a function, the input parameters are like base attributes and output parameters are like derived attributes. Thus, the proposition that an instance is indeed a member of a function (or class) is decidable iff the function terminates for a given input (though termination is still undecidable). Further, if such class membership is computable for each instance (of a given class) in the persistent store, then the subclass relationship is also computable.[5]

[3]Computing the subsumption relationship is not decidable for all term subsumption languages, most notably KL-ONE [14].

[4]This ontologic nature of databases is in stark contrast to the role of persistent types played in programming languages.

[5]Since any instance of f must also satisfy the constraints of its superclass g due to inheritance, mutual inconsistency will be detected at least for those instances existing in the store. Additionally, this model will work in cases where the domain of an attribute is a function.

Let f be a function and $\mathcal{E}[f]$ be its extension. Based on our above discussion, the extension is a finite set in the store. However, the notion of temporary instance creation provides us with a means to make arbitrary computations. Thus, there are no restrictions on what values may be persistent (as is often the case in many DBPLs), i.e., a function can also have instances in the persistent store just like any other class. The keyword **function** serves only one purpose, namely, that the class (or function) in question is precluded from participating in the class taxonomy. This is because we do not know what a taxonomy of functions might mean. The above model for inheritance is different from those described in [5, 15, 16, 19] because we provide an extensional account of inheritance rather than intensional.

Since the subclass relationship can be computed based on the above approach, the main argument against it would be a combinatorial explosion. However, coupled with our execution model, it conceptually provides a methodology to deal with the problem of procedural attachments in frame-based languages. As mentioned earlier, this approach should be contrasted with term subsumption languages. However, we can still use the same classification algorithm to build a taxonomy of functions. The ability to define a taxonomy of functions might be of use in functional abstractions used in simulation applications.

6.5 Equality, Assignment and Modify

It is very important to be able to define equality between expressions in a programming language. We have already seen equality in chapter 3 for objects, and we have seen in chapters 5 and 6 how equality is overloaded. This issue is made poignant in section 6.3, where we discuss how the notion of temporary instance creation allows us to give an operational equivalence to the semantics of a class and function. Equality is different from the assignment and **modify** operators, in the sense that it is not destructive. The assignment and **modify** operators have a very similar semantics—actually the assignment operator is syntactic sugar for **modify**. For example, let i be an instance and a_j its attributes. Then $\{\textbf{modify}.i \mid a_1 = v_1 \textbf{ and} \ldots \textbf{and } a_n = v_n\}$ is equivalent to a sequence of assignments: $i.a_1 := v_1; \ldots; i.a_n := v_n$; From an implementation viewpoint, the **modify** operation would be less expensive to compile than the sequence of assignments because the context (that is, the LHS) is evaluated only once in the former case, while it would be evaluated n times in the latter. Consider another example: $s := x \equiv \{\textbf{modify}.s \mid \textbf{self} = x\}$ or $o.a := v \equiv \{\textbf{modify}.o \mid a = x\}$. The LHS of an assignment must denote an attribute name, and the expression on the RHS must be of the same type as the type of the attribute on the LHS. If s in $s := x$ refers to a non-persistent value (such as a transient attribute), then only the run-time environment is updated. On the other hand, if s refers to a persistent value, then the database (that is, persistent store) as well as the run-time environment are updated.

6.6 Scope of Identifiers

We have already examined the scope of identifiers in a set expression in chapter 4. We saw that the context of a set expression determines the scope of identifiers. The only way to override the scope imposed by the context is to use the **prev** operator. To understand the scope of identifiers when they occur in a function definition, we first need to understand how the user interacts with Voltaire. While details of such interactions are deferred to section 7.1, we briefly introduce the **eval** command here. Given that a user has loaded some database and a corresponding schema into the Voltaire environment, s/he can issue various commands. The **eval** command takes a set expression as an argument and evaluates it against the currently active database. Recall that functions are triggered via set expressions. For example, to compute the factorial of 6, the user would say **eval** {fact.f | n = 6}, or the cost of a pump can computed by issuing the command **eval** {ComputeCost.resultcost | partname = "pump" }. This is known as the outermost layer of evaluation.

When a function is triggered by a set expression from the outermost layer of evaluation, it is passed an initial environment which consists of the identifiers bound to their respective values on RHS of the set expression. Other attributes (or parameters) of the function are bound as the computation progresses. The database schema is treated as a global declaration. It is useful to think of the database as an environment which maps classes to instances. Thus, the context of any set expression is now decided with respect to this global environment (i.e., the database) and the local environment.[6] When computing the value of an identifier, the values in the local environment take precedence. Once we have moved from the Voltaire environment to an inner level of computation, the run-time environment looks much different due to the notion of temporary instance creation and the **prev** operator.

The run-time environment is $Renv = Self \times Cenv \times Penv$, where $Self$ denotes the currently active record, $Cenv$ denotes the currently active environment and $Penv$ denotes the calling (or previous) environment. Further, $Self = Cenv = Penv = Env = Id \rightarrow Denotable\_Value$. $Self$ essentially maintains a copy of the currently active record against which the **self** operator is evaluated. This is required when a query is being evaluated within a function call. For example, consider {Person | age < 50}. If the class *Person* has n instances, and the ith instance is being evaluated, then $Self$ is used to denote that instance. Any modification to the current environment is reflected in $Self$, though the reverse case is not true. Similarly, the **prev** operator is evaluated with respect to $Penv$. $Cenv$ behaves in the usual manner. It must

[6]Apropos, it should be clear that the context is decided with respect to the global environment or database for all the examples of chapter 4.

be noted that each time a set expression is encountered in the function body, it is evaluated with a new run-time environment. We do not allow dot expressions of the form **prev.prev.***identifier*, since that would require the run-time environment to maintain information about all the previous environments, one for each level of nesting.

6.7 Function Composition

As mentioned earlier, Voltaire is a first order language. However, the extent of a function is a denotable value (which can also be persistent). Therefore, an element belonging to the extent of a function can be embedded in data structures, passed as a parameter, or returned as a value. Therefore, function names are valid identifiers in a dot expression. Thus, the dot operator also denotes function composition. For example, let f_1 and f_2 denote two functions and i_1, o_1 and i_2, o_2 denote their respective attributes (input and output parameters). Then,

$$\{f_1.f_2.o_2 \mid f_1.i_1 = v_1 \wedge f_2.i_2 = o_1\}$$

is a valid expression, and is equivalent to $f_2 \circ f_1$.[7] (Strictly speaking, the two expressions are equivalent after an implicit coercion in the sense discussed below.) It should be expected that the subexpression $f_2.f_1$ is valid if and only if f_1 and f_2 are isomorphisms. This means that even though $f_1.f_2$ may have a denotable value, it does not imply that $f_2.f_1$ will also have a denotable value, unless the two functions are isomorphisms. The reason why this is to be expected is that the extent of a function is exactly its graph. Further, the above set expression could also have been equivalently written as

$$\{f_2.o_2 \mid i_2 = \{f_1.o_1 \mid i_1 = v_1\}\} .$$

[7]Note that $\{f_1.f_2 \mid f_1.i_1 = v_1 \wedge f_2.i_2 = o_1\}$ is not equivalent to $f_2 \circ f_1$, since the set expression returns a reference to an instance of f_2, rather than the value o_2.

Thus, even though Voltaire has a first order syntax, an element belonging to the extent of a function can be embedded in data structures, passed as a parameter, or returned as a value.

It might be useful to list the various forms of the dot operator, each of which are mutually consistent.

1. $c.a$ denotes the set of values of the attribute a of class c, such that a is selected from each instance $i \in c$. This can equivalently denote function evaluation as discussed in section 6.3.

2. $f.o$ denotes the value of parameter o of a function f, which is the result of evaluating f. Again, this can equivalently denote set evaluation if f has a persistent extent, as discussed in section 6.1.

3. $i.a$ denotes the usual field selection for records if i is an instance (of a class or function), having the attribute a. There is one important difference, namely, in our case, $i.a$ will return a singleton set whose element is the value of a for i.

If s is an identifier of type t, then $s := i.a$ is legal, because there is an implicit coercion. If $i.a$ evaluates to a singleton set with the element v, namely, $\{v\}$, it is coerced to v since $\{v\} \notin \mathcal{I}(t)$. However, $s := c.a$ can be valid if and only $c.a$ evaluates to a singleton set. Since this can be known only at run-time, it would limit the usefulness of any static type checking. Therefore, we impose the restriction that the above expression is valid if and only if s has $\{t\}$. The rule for $f.o$ is similar to that of $i.a$.

CHAPTER 7
THE VOLTAIRE ENVIRONMENT AND ITS SEMANTICS

7.1 Interacting with the Voltaire Environment

The user must first enter the Voltaire environment before a database is loaded and computations are made against it. At this level of evaluation, the environment is interactive—it prompts the user for input and reports the result of computations. The user can begin making computations after loading a schema and a database by using the **load_db** command. If the schema and/or database do not exist, then the system returns a message warning the user that the schema and the database have been initialized to **null**, so that any computations other than **new_c** and **new_i** will fail. The **new_c** command is used to create either a new class or a new function. This class is inserted in the schema at the appropriate place, and corresponding modifications are made in the database. For example, if a new class has superclass c_{sup}, then it is possible that some instances of c_{sup} may migrate to the new class. Effectively, this implies a coercion on the type of all instances that migrate from c_{sup} to the new class. The **new_i** command is used to create new instances. The user should not specify the unique object identifier since the system automatically assigns one to the new object being created. However, the user needs to specify the parent class(es) of the new instance along with all the attribute value pairs. The system will then check if the new instance satisfies all the structural and behavioral constraints of each parent class. In order to ensure type safeness, the type of each instance is verified at the time of creation, as well as when loading a given database with respect to a given schema.

Once a populated database exists within the environment, various other computations can be made. The **eval** command is used to evaluate either a function or a query expression. The LHS of a set expression (which defines the context within which the rest of the expression is to be evaluated) can only refer to names defined in the schema. The reason why a single **eval** command suffices is because classes and functions have an equivalent semantics. For example, consider {fact.f | n = 6} and {Student.name | ss# = 111222333}. The result of a query is tabular. For example, the result of the query { Dept[name].Course[title].Section[textbook] | Course.c# ≤ 6000 **and** Course.c# < 7000 } is a table which can be described as a set of objects such that each object has the type $\langle name : \mathbf{string}, \{\langle title : \mathbf{string}, textbook : \{\mathbf{string}\}\rangle\}\rangle$, given that a Department offers many courses and that each course has many sections (each of which may follow different textbooks). The result of the factorial function would be the value 720.

Since we have adopted a lazy evaluation mode for enforcing integrity constraints, it is possible that instances belonging to certain classes are modified and the database can then result in an inconsistent state. To find out which instances of a given class cause the database to result in an inconsistent state, one can use the **check** <classname> command. If the name of the class is specified as *Any*, then each and every class in the schema is checked to discover inconsistent instances. The result is displayed as an object graph (that is, linear span-tree), with a question mark indicating the source of trouble. For example, an instance i_0 may have an attribute a_0 which refers to an instance i_k of another class, possibly through many levels of indirection. Now, if it is the case that i_k is either nonexistent or inconsistent, then a question mark would appear:

$$i_0 \xrightarrow{a_0} \cdots \xrightarrow{a_{k-1}} i_k \ (?)$$

It is trivial to generate such a graph by computing the span-tree of i_0 as discussed in section 3.4.1. An alternative form of this command is **check** <classname>: <set_expr>. This command checks if the instances returned by the set expression are members of a given class (note that membership implies consistency). For example, **check** Department: {Student.advisor.Faculty.dept | Faculty.salary ≥ 50000} will check only those instances returned by the set expression rather than all instances of class *Department* for consistency. Also, the resulting object graph will begin with an instance of class *Department*. This command is also useful in finding out nonmembers of a class. For example, **check** RA: {TA} will result in a set of instances of *RA* that are not in *TA*. This information can then be used to coerce the type *RA* on instances of *TA* (this is legal since we support multiple inheritance).

The **delete_i** <set_expr> command is used to delete all instances returned as the result of evaluating the set expression. This delete operation should be used with caution since it will blindly delete all objects returned by the set expression without regard for the consistency of the database. However, it is useful in order to delete inconsistent objects determined by the **check** command. The semantics of this delete operator is identical to that when it appears in a function for the case of persistent objects.

Transcripts of a session (or a portion of the session) with Voltaire can be saved in a file by using the **save** command. The user can eventually **quit** a session, which has the effect of closing the database and returning to the operating system. Since each command is considered as an atomic transaction, the effects of a successful execution are permanently reflected in the database. For example, if a function for increasing *Faculty* salaries by 10% is executed by the **eval** command, then all instances of the class *Faculty* are updated upon successful execution of the function, and will be reflected the next time the database is loaded.

7.2 A Denotational Semantics for Voltaire

In decreasing level of abstraction, there are three complementary methodologies for defining the semantics of a programming language, namely, axiomatic, denotational and operational semantics [47]. The last method uses an interpreter to define a language. The meaning of a program is the evaluation history that the interpreter produces when it interprets the program. In the denotational semantics approach, a program is directly mapped to its meaning, called its denotation. A *valuation* function maps a program directly to its denotation, which is a mathematical value such as a number or function. With an axiomatic semantics, properties about language constructs are defined, expressed with axioms and inference rules from symbolic logic.

A denotational description of a programming language consists of an abstract syntax, a set of semantic domains along with their operators, and a valuation function. A semantic domain along with its set of operators is called a semantic algebra. Before the valuation function is defined, we must define appropriate semantic algebras for primitive domains such as numbers and boolean, compound domains such as sets, lists and records, and other complex domains such as run-time environments and memory stores. The valuation function takes an abstract syntax tree of the program and maps it onto its meaning with the help of these semantic algebras.

There are many styles of denotational semantics. Two important styles are direct and continuation semantics. Direct semantics definitions tend to use lower-order expressions, and emphasize the compositional structure of a language. For example, the equation $\mathcal{E}[\![E_1 + E_2]\!] = \lambda e.\mathcal{E}[\![E_1]\!]e \; plus \; \mathcal{E}[\![E_2]\!]e$ gives a simple definition of *side-effect* free addition, that is, there is no notion of sequencing in this definition. Sequencing is an entirely operational notion. However, sequencing is an important control structure in all imperative languages. The semantic argument that models control is called a *continuation*. As an analogy, the activation record stack of a programming language translator contains the sequencing information that "drives" the evaluation of a program. Thus, the above example can be rewritten in the continuation style as follows:

$$\mathcal{E}[\![E_1 + E_2]\!] = \lambda e.\lambda k.\ \mathcal{E}[\![E_1]\!]e(\lambda n_1.\ \mathcal{E}[\![E_2]\!]e\ (\lambda n_2.\ k(n_1\ plus\ n_2)))$$

where e is the run-time environment argument and k is the continuation or control argument. An important advantage of using a continuation is that abstractions in the semantic equations are nonstrict. This is because the continuation effectively captures the notion of "rest of the program" (in an expression-oriented language, the program is an expression); thus the remainder of the program (denoted by k) is never reached when an infinite loop is encountered. Though it is often possible to show the equivalence (or more precisely, congruence) between a direct and continuation style semantics for a given language, it is difficult.

As discussed in chapter 6, the definition of a transaction is still an area of on-going research for object-based database languages. We believe that one effective way to study various possible definitions of a transaction is by defining a continuation style semantics for the language. The central idea is that a valuation function then maps a database program directly onto a transaction. One of the original targets of this research was to define a transaction with the help of a continuation semantics. While a concise continuation semantics to define transactions has managed to elude us, we have been partially successful in defining a direct semantics for Voltaire. The concrete syntax is defined in Appendix B, the abstract syntax is defined in Appendix C, and the denotational semantics is defined in Appendix D. We follow the notation found in [47].

7.3 Implementation Strategy

Our implementation strategy is shown in Figure 7.1. A Voltaire schema (consisting of class and function definitions) is first translated by a parser into an abstract syntax tree (AST). This AST is then analyzed by a semantic processor for consistency, and possible optimization. If any syntax errors are detected, then they are reported to the user at this level. If there are no errors, then another abstract syntax tree (AST*) is generated. The run-time environment takes a request from the user and executes it with respect to AST*. Effectively, the run-time environment recursively walks the abstract syntax tree (AST*) to execute the user request. The main advantage of this implementation strategy is that multiple optimization strategies may be pursued independently, but in a coherent fashion. For example, the semantic processor can exploit different optimization strategies to convert AST to AST*, such as algebraic rewrites. Also, the run-time environment can exploit another set of optimizations in which access from the persistent store is more efficient. A single user request is treated as an atomic transaction.

If the user modifies the current schema in the middle of a session with the environment, then any such change must be reflected. Since the run-time environment will only reference (and therefore modify AST*), there must be another mechanism to translate the changes made to AST* back into Voltaire code. Thus, when the user quits the environment, AST* is translated back into Voltaire code by the deparser.

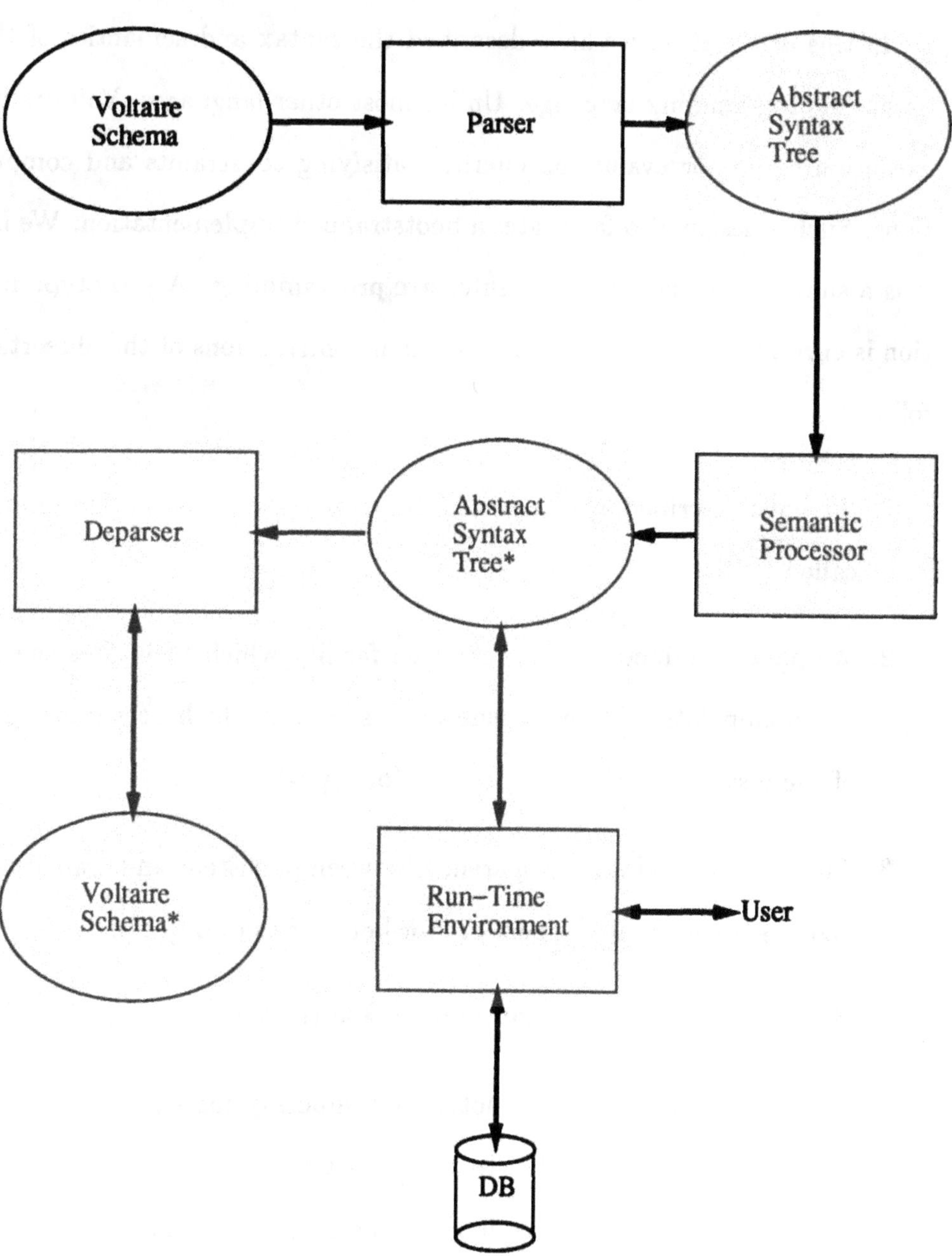

Figure 7.1. Implementation of Voltaire

CHAPTER 8
CONCLUSIONS AND FUTURE RESEARCH

In this dissertation we have described the syntax and semantics of the Voltaire database programming language. Unlike most other languages, Voltaire has a single execution model for evaluating queries, satisfying constraints and computing functions. Such a design also facilitates a bootstrapped implementation. We believe that it is a suitable language for data intensive programming. A prototype implementation is currently being completed. The main contributions of this dissertation are as follows:

1. We have described a set-oriented, imperative database programming language called Voltaire.

2. We have described a data definition facility which facilitates sharing of data and manipulation of heterogeneous sets, and in which persistence is a property of the instances rather than classes (or types).

3. The system provides transparency between persistent and transient objects by defining a single set of operators for both kinds of objects.

4. We have designed the language in an additive or bootstrapping fashion.

5. We have discussed how the notion of temporary instance creation allows us to give an equivalent semantics to classes and functions, which seemed necessary to have a single model of execution for querying, enforcing integrity and computing functions.

6. We have given a formal definition to the object model of Voltaire, which accounts for behavior as well as the extent of a type. Thus, it provides a uniform semantics for the persistent store (i.e., the database) and the run–time environment by making it possible to statically type check expressions.

7. We have also given a partial denotational semantics, defining the main features of Voltaire.

While the fact that the sequential order of constraints is significant may be considered as a limitation, we placed that restriction to avoid traditional computational overhead associated with constraints. Also, we can now compute a function which consists of evaluating or satisfying a sequence of constraints. Since functions and classes are equivalent, they can be thought of as views (and likewise, the output parameters of the function as derived attributes). The values of derived attributes are not stored, but are computed only upon demand. This adds to run–time overhead, but guarantees that the user will always obtain correct results.

While our type system has certain useful properties, the type expressions are not as powerful as in, say, Machiavelli. For example, we have not considered variant records; polymorphism is ad hoc in terms of operator overloading, implicit coercion and inheritance. It is an open question whether we can define a static type discipline that is truly polymorphic, but also supports sharing of heterogeneous data. Advanced issues such as exception handling or versioning may be addressed to enhance the language. There are at least two directions for future research that appear promising:

1. Since the set expressions in Voltaire are very similar to those in SETL, it would be interesting to investigate the possibility of extending SETL to make it a polymorphic, strongly typed database programming language with static type checking.

2. Extend the denotational description of Voltaire to a continuation style of semantics, which could then be used to study the notion of transactions for DBPLs.
3. Extend the type system of Voltaire to define a type inferencing mechanism that would eliminate the need the pre–define transient attributes.

APPENDIX A
UNIVERSITY SCHEMA

```
class Person defined
superclasses Any
subclasses Student, Teacher
attributes
    ss#: integer
    name: string

class Student defined
superclasses Person
subclasses Grad, Undergrad
attributes
    gpa: real
    major: Dept
    sections: set Section
    transcripts: set Transcript
    total_work: integer
    total_credit: integer
    job_hours: integer
    leisure_time: integer
    visa_status: integer
constraints
    total_credit = sum {sections.course.credit_hours };
    total_work = total_credit + job_hours;
    leisure_time = 80 − total_work;
    leisure_time > 20;
    if visa_status = "F-1" then job_hours ≤ 20;

class Grad defined
superclasses Student
subclasses RA, TA
attributes
    advisor: Faculty
    committee: set Faculty
    status: string
```

```
    course_work: string
    degree_req: string
    thesis_option: integer
constraints
    if exists thesis_option then advisor and advisor in committee;
    for all { section.course.c# | c# ≥ 5000 };
    if status = "full-time" then total_credit ≥ 12;
    if course_work = "done" and thesis_status = "defended" and
        count { committee.Faculty | Faculty.Dept includes Dept } ≥ 2
        then degree_req = "fulfilled";

class Undergrad defined
superclasses Student
attributes
    minor: Dept

class Teacher defined
superclasses Person
subclasses Faculty, TA
attributes
    degree: string

class Faculty defined
superclasses Teacher
attributes
    books: string
    specialty: string
    advises: set Grad

class TA defined
superclasses Teacher, Grad
attributes
    supervisor: Faculty

    class RA defined
    superclasses Grad
attributes
    project: string

class Section defined
superclasses Any
attributes
```

```
    section#: string
    room#: string
    textbook: string
    taught_by: Teacher
    course: Course
    enrollment: set Student

class Course defined
superclasses Any
attributes
    c#: string
    title: string
    credit_hours: integer
    prereqs: set Course
    sections: set Section
    enrollment: set Student
    dept: Dept

class Dept defined
superclasses Any
attributes
    name: string
    college: string
    students: set Student
    courses_offered: set Course

class Transcript defined
superclasses Any
attributes
    grade: integer
    course: Course
    student: Student

class Advising defined
superclasses Any
attributes
    startdate: string
    faculty: Faculty
    student: Student
```

APPENDIX B
CONCRETE SYNTAX

I. A BNF for the Data Definition Sublanguage

<db> ::= <schema> <database>
<schema> ::= <class>+
<database> ::= <instance>+

<class> ::= **class** <classname> (**defined** | **function**)
[**superclasses** <superclass>+]
[**subclasses** <subclass>+]
[**instances** <ref>+]
[**attributes** <attr_domain>+]
[**transients** <attr_domain>+]
[**constraints:** <B>]

<instance> ::= **instance** <ref> [<parent_class>+]
[**attributes** <attr_value>+]

<attr_domain> ::= <attr_name> : <domain> | <attr_name> = <value>

<domain> ::= **nil** | **any** | **string** | **integer** | **real** | <class_name> |
set <domain>+ | **list** <domain>+ | **tuple** <attr_domain>+

<attr_value> ::= <attr_name> = <value>

<value> ::= **null** | <ref> | <integer> | <real> | "<string>" |
<set_value> | <list_value> | <tuple_value>
<set_value> ::= { <value>+ }
<list_value> ::= (<value>+)
<tuple_value> ::= [<attr_value>+]

<superclass> ::= <class_name>
<subclass> ::= <class_name>
<parent_class> ::= <class_name>
<class_name> ::= <Identifier>
<attr_name> ::= <Identifier>

II. Some Data Manipulation Operators

<dml-ops> ::= <new> | <modify> | <delete>

<new> ::= <dot_expr> = { **new.**<classname> | <attr_value>+ } |
<dot_expr> = { **new.**<classname> | <Identifier> }
<modify> ::= { **modify.**<dot_expr> | <Bool> }
<delete> ::= { **delete.**<dot_expr> | <Bool> }

III. Query Sublanguage

<set_expr> ::= { <E> | <Bool> } | { <E> } | <E> |
<agg_op> <set_expr>

<Bool> ::= (<Bool>) | **not** <Bool> | < Bool$_1$ > **or** < Bool$_2$ > |
< Bool$_1$ > **and** < Bool$_2$ > | < E$_1$ > <rel-op> < E$_2$ > |
< E$_1$ > = < E$_2$ > | **forall** <E> : <Bool> |
exists <E> | **dbexists** <E>

<E> ::= <dot_expr> | − <term> | <term> | <term> <add-op> <E>

<dot_expr> ::= <I> | <I>.<dot_expr> | < I$_1$ > [< I$_2$ >+] |
< I$_1$ > [< I$_2$ >+].<dot_expr>

<term> ::= <factor> | <factor> <multiply-op> <term>

<factor> ::= <ref> | <integer> | <real> | "<string>" |
<set_expr> | <set_constants>

<set_constants> ::= { <ref>+ } | { <integer>+ } | { <real>+ } |
{ <string>+ } | { <Identifier>+ }

<agg_op> ::= **count** | **sum** | **avg** | **min** | **max**

<rel-op> ::= ≠ | ≤ | ≥ | < | > |**in**|**includes**
<add-op> ::= + | −
<multiply-op> ::= × | ÷ | **mod** | **div**

<I> ::= **prev** | **next** | **self** | **head** | **tail** | <Identifiers>

IV. Additive Constraint Sublanguage

<B> ::= < B_1 > ; < B_2 > | <Bool> | < $Comm_1$ >

< $Comm_1$ > ::= **if** <Bool> **then** <B> **endif** |
if <Bool> **then** < B_1 > **else** < B_2 > **endif**

V. Additive Programming Sublanguage

< $Comm_2$ > ::= < $Comm_1$ > | <Assignment> | <Loop> | <dml-ops> | <io>

<Assignment> ::= <dot_expr> := <set_expr>

<Loop> ::= <Iterator> | <While>
<Iterator> ::= **for each** <I> **in** <set_expr> **do** <B> **enddo**
<While> ::= **while** <Bool> **do** <B> **enddo**

<io> ::= <open> | <close> | <print> | <read>

VI. Environment

<Sess_Op> ::= **new_c** <class> | **new_i** <instance> | **eval** <set_expr> |
<Session> ::= **load_db** <db> <Sess_Op>+

<Sess_Op> ::=**new_c** <class> | **new_i** <instance> | **eval** <set_expr> |
script <file_name> | **check** <classname> |
check <classname>: <set_expr> | **quit**
savein <file_name> | **delete_i** <set_expr> |

APPENDIX C
ABSTRACT SYNTAX

Voltaire ::= **load_db** Sc Db S

S ::= $S_1; S_2$ | **new_c** Cl | **new_i** Ins | **eval** SE |
script Fn | **check** Cn |
check Cn SE | **quit**
savein Fn | **delete_i** SE |

Cl ::= **class** Cn (**defined** | **function**)
[**superclasses** Sup
[**subclasses** Sub
[**instances** Rf]
[**attributes** AD]
[**transients** AD]
[**constraints:** B]

AD ::= An : D | An = V

D ::= **nil** | **any** | **string** | **integer** | **real** | Cn |
set D | **list** D | **tuple** AD

Ins ::= **instance** Rf [Cn+] [**attributes** AV]

AV ::= An = V

V ::= **null** | Rf | Int | R | St | SV | TV

SV ::= {V+}
TV ::= [AV+]

Sc ::= Cl+
Db ::= Ins+

Sup ::= Cn
Sub ::= Cn
Cn ::= Ide

An ::= Ide

B ::= B_1;B_2 | Bo | C

C ::= **if** Bo **then** B **endif** | **if** Bo **then** B_1 **else** B_2 **endif**
A | L | DML | IO

Bo ::= (Bo) | **not** Bo | Bo_1 **or** Bo_2 | Bo_1 **and** Bo_2
| E_1 Rel E_2 | $E_1 = E_2$ |
forall E : Bo | **exists** E | **dbexists** E

E ::= −T | T | T Add E | DE

T ::= F | F Mul T
F ::= Rf | Int | R | "St" | SV | SE

Agg ::= **count** | **sum** | **avg** | **min** | **max**
Rel ::= ≠ | ≤ | ≥ | < | > | **in** | **includes**
Add ::= + | −
Mul ::= × | ÷ | **mod** | **div**

I ::= **prev** | **self** | **head** | **tail** | Ide

DML ::= New | Mod | Del
New ::= DE = { **new**.Cn | AV+ } | DE = { **new**.Cn | Ide }
Mod ::= { **modify**.DE | Bo }
Del ::= { **delete**.DE | Bo }

DE ::= I | I.DE | I_1 [I_2+] | I_1 [I_2+].DE

SE ::= { E | Bo } | { E } | E | Agg SE

A ::= DE := SE

L ::= It | W
It ::= **for each** Ide **in** SE **do** B **enddo**
W ::= **while** Bo **do** B **enddo**

IO ::= Open | Close | Print | Read

APPENDIX D
DENOTATIONAL SEMANTICS

Semantic Algebras

1. *Integer, Real, String, Boolean, Identifier.*

2. Denotable Values:

$$Dv = Integers + Reals + String + Boolean + Set + List + Tuple + Ref + Nil + Any + Location + Errvalue$$

where $Errvalue = Unit$

$List = Set = Dv+$

$Tuple = Id \rightarrow Dv = Environment$

3. Expressible Values:

$$Ev = Integers + Reals + String + Boolean + Set + List + Tuple + Ref + Nil + Any + Errvalue$$

4. Storable Values:

$$Sv = Integers + Reals + String + Boolean + Set + List + Tuple + Ref + Nil + Any$$

5. Storage Locations:

Domain $l \in Locn$

Operations:

- *first_locn:Locn*
- *next_locn:Locn → Locn*
- *equal_locn:Locn → Locn → Tr*
- *lessthan_locn:Locn → Locn → Tr*

6. Stack–Based Store:

   Domain *Store = (Locn → Sv) × Locn*

   Operations:

   - *access: Locn →Store →(Sv + Errvalue)*

     $$access = \lambda l.\lambda(map, top).l\ lessthan\_locn\ top \rightarrow \mathrm{in}Sv(map\ l) \mid \mathrm{in}Errvalue()$$

   - *update: Locn →Sv →Store →PostStore*

     $$update = \lambda l.\lambda v.\lambda(map, top).l\ lessthan\_locn\ top \rightarrow \mathrm{in}OK([l \mapsto v]map, top) \mid \mathrm{in}Err(map, top)$$

   - *mark_locn: Store →Locn*

     $$mark\_locn = \lambda(map, top).top$$

   - *allocate_locn: Store →Locn × PostStore*

     $$allocate\_locn = \lambda(map, top).(top, inOK(map, next\_locn(top)))$$

   - *deallocate_locns: Locn →Store →PostStore*

     $$deallocate\_locns = \lambda l.\lambda(map, top).((l\ lessthan\_locn\ top) \vee (l\ equal\_locn\ top)) \rightarrow inOK(map, l) \mid inErr(map, top)$$

7. Environment:

Domain $Env = Environment = Id \to Ev$

Operations:

- *emptyenv: Env*

  $emptyenv = \lambda i.(inErrvalue())$

- *accessenv: Id $\to$ Env $\to$ Dv*

  $accessenv = \lambda i.\lambda e.e(i)$

- *updateenv: Id $\to$ Dv $\to$ Env $\to$ Env*

  $updateenv = \lambda i.\lambda d.\lambda e.([i \mapsto d]e)$

8. PostStore: Run-time store, labeled with status of computation

Domain $p \in PostStore = OK + Err$

where $OK = Err = Store$

Operations:

- *return: Store $\to$ PostStore*

  $return = \lambda s.inOK(s)$

- *signalerr: Store $\to$ PostStore*

  $signalerr = \lambda s.inErr(s)$

- *check: (Store $\to$ (Env $\times$ PostStore)) $\to$ (PostStore $\to$ (Env $\times$ PostStore))*

  $$\begin{aligned} check\ f = \underline{\lambda} p.\ & cases\ p\ of \\ & \text{is}OK(s) \to (f\ s) \mid \\ & \text{is}Err(s) \to p \\ & \text{end} \end{aligned}$$

9. Voltaire Database:

   $Clunction = Class + Function$

   $Class = ClassName \rightarrow ClassStructure$

   $Function = FunctionName \rightarrow ClassStructure$

   $ClassStructure = AD^* \times TR^* \times Constraints$

   Domain $\tau_1 \in C\_Ref\_Table = Name \rightarrow Ref^*$

   $ClassHier = ClassName \times ClassName \rightarrow Boolean$

   $Instance = Ref \rightarrow (Aname \rightarrow Sv)^*$

   Domain $\tau_2 \in I\_C\_Table = Ref \rightarrow Name^*$

   Domain $\sigma \in Schema = Class \times C\_Ref\_Table \times ClassHier$

   Domain $\delta \in Database = Instance \times I\_C\_Table$

   Domain $\gamma \in DB = Schema \times Database$

   Domain $AD = AttributeDomain = Aname \times ClassName$

   Domain $TR = Transients = Aname \times ClassName$

   $Constraints = B$

<u>Valuation Functions</u>

1. Voltaire: S $\rightarrow Db \rightarrow Db$

   Voltaire[[**load_db** Sc Db S]]=
   $\lambda(\gamma)$. **let** $\gamma' =$
   $load_\delta[\![Db]\!](load_\sigma[\![Sc]\!](init_\sigma), init_\delta)$
   in OP[[S]](γ')

   - $init_\sigma : Sc$

$$init_\sigma = \lambda().\textbf{let}\ \text{empty\_classes} = \text{nil}\ \textbf{and}$$
$$\text{init\_hier} = \lambda.F\ \textbf{and}$$
$$init_{\tau_1} = \text{nil}\ \textbf{in}$$
$$(empty\_classes, init\_hier, init_{\tau_1})$$

- $init_\delta : Db$

$$init_\delta = \lambda().\textbf{let}\ \text{empty\_instances} = \text{nil}\ \textbf{and}$$
$$init_{\tau_2} = \text{nil}\ \textbf{in}$$
$$(empty\_classes, init_{\tau_2})$$

- $load_\sigma : Sc \rightarrow \sigma \rightarrow \sigma$

$$load_\sigma[\![Sc]\!] = \lambda\sigma.\ Sc = nil \rightarrow \sigma \mid$$
$$load_\sigma[\![\textbf{tail}\ Sc]\!](\text{Create\_Class}[\![\textbf{head}\ Sc]\!]\sigma)$$

- $load_\delta : Db \rightarrow \gamma \rightarrow \gamma$

$$load_\delta[\![Db]\!] = \lambda\gamma.\ Db = nil \rightarrow \gamma \mid$$
$$load_\delta[\![\textbf{tail}\ Db]\!](\text{Create\_Instance}[\![\textbf{head}\ Db]\!]\delta)$$

- Create_Class: $Cl \rightarrow \sigma \rightarrow \sigma$

Create_Class [[(N, Class_Type, Sup, Sub, R, A, T, Constraints)]]=
$\lambda(c, \tau_1, h)$. **cases** Class_Type of
"Class" $\rightarrow([N \mapsto (A, T, Constraints)]c, \tau_1, h)\mid$
"Function" $\rightarrow([N \mapsto (A, T, Constraints)]c, \tau_1, h)\mid$
end

- Create_Instance: $Ins \rightarrow DB \rightarrow DB$

Create_Instance [[(Ref, P, AV)]]= $\lambda(\sigma, (i, \tau_2))$.
let $i' = [Ref \mapsto conv\_AV(\text{AV})]i$ **in**
$update_\gamma(Ref, P, (\sigma, (i', \tau_2)))$

- $update_\gamma$: Ref $\times$ Name* $\times \gamma \rightarrow \gamma$

$$update_\gamma = \lambda(r, p, \gamma).p = nil \rightarrow \gamma \mid$$
$$update_\gamma(r, \textbf{tail}\ p, rec\_upd_\gamma(r, \textbf{head}\ p, \gamma))$$

- $rec\_upd_\gamma : Ref \times Name \rightarrow DB \rightarrow DB$

$$rec\_upd_\gamma = \lambda(r, p).\lambda(\sigma, \delta).member\_i\_c(r, p) \rightarrow$$
$$(update\_\tau_1(r, p, \sigma), update\_\tau_2(r, p, \delta)) \mid (\sigma, \delta)$$

- $update\_\tau_1 : Ref \times Name \times Schema \times Schema$

  $$update\_\tau_1 = \lambda(r, p, (c, \tau_1, h)).\\ (c, [p \mapsto \tau_1(p)\textbf{cons}\ r]\tau_1, h)$$

- $update\_\tau_2 : Ref \times Name \times Database \times Database$

  $$update\_\tau_2 = \lambda(r, p, (i, \tau_2)).\\ (i, [r \mapsto \tau_2(r)\textbf{cons}\ p]\tau_2)$$

- *member_i_c: Ref* $\times$ *Name* $\rightarrow$*Boolean*

  This function returns true if the instance denoted by Ref is a member of the class denoted by Name.

- conv_AV: AV $\rightarrow$(An $\rightarrow$Sv)*

2. OP: S $\rightarrow Db \rightarrow Db$
   $OP[\![S_1; S_2]\!] = OP[\![S_2]\!](OP[\![S_1]\!])$
   $OP[\![\textbf{new\_c}\ Cl]\!] = \lambda(\sigma, \delta).\ (Create\_class\ Cl\ \sigma,\ \delta)$

   $$OP[\![\textbf{new\_i} < \text{P}, \text{AV} >]\!] = \lambda\gamma.\ \textbf{let}\ R = invent\_Ref\\ \textbf{in}\ \text{Create\_instance}\ < \text{R}, \text{P}, \text{AV} > \gamma$$

   OP[[**eval** SE]]= OP[[**eval** {E | Bo}]]

For the time being, we only consider the following forms of function evaluation:

$\{f.o \mid i_1 = E_1\ \textbf{and} \ldots \textbf{and}\ i_n = E_n\}$ or $\{f \mid i_1 = E_1\ \textbf{and} \ldots \textbf{and}\ i_n = E_n\}$

$$\begin{aligned} OP[\![\textbf{eval}\ SE]\!] = \lambda\gamma.\textbf{let}\ a = get\_anchor(SE)\ \textbf{in} \\ \textbf{cases}\ a\ \text{of} \\ \text{is}Function(f) \rightarrow \\ eval\_fn\ get\_constr(f)\ init\_env(\text{SE}, f, \gamma)\ \gamma \mid \\ \text{is}Class(c) \rightarrow eval\_query(\text{SE}, c)\ \gamma \mid \\ \text{is}Errvalue(e) \rightarrow \text{in}Errvalue(e) \\ \textbf{end} \end{aligned}$$

- get_constr: Name $\rightarrow$B

  $$\begin{aligned} \text{get\_constr} = \lambda k.\ isFunction(k) \rightarrow (function\ k)\downarrow 4 \mid \\ isClass(k) \rightarrow (class\ k)\downarrow 4 \mid \\ in\text{Errvalue}(k) \end{aligned}$$

- *init_env: SE →Name →Db →(Env × PostStore)*

  $init\_env[\![\{E|Bo\}]\!] = \lambda n.\lambda\gamma.$
  let (e,p) = *getstorage emptyenv* $(getattr(n), gettrans(n))$ **in**
  create_temp_inst $[\![Bo]\!](e,p)$

- getattr: Name →AD*

  $getattr = \lambda n.\ \text{is}Function(n) \rightarrow (function\ n)\downarrow 1\ |$
  $\text{is}Class(n) \rightarrow (class\ n)\downarrow 1\ |$
  $\text{inErrvalue}(n)$

- *gettrans: Name →TR**

  $\text{gettrans} = \lambda n.\ isFunction(n) \rightarrow (function\ n)\downarrow 2\ |$
  $\text{is}Class(n) \rightarrow (class\ n)\downarrow 2\ |$
  $\text{inErrvalue}(n)$

- *create_temp_inst: Bo →DB →(Env × PostStore) →(Env × PostStore)*

  Basically, *Env* will always have an identifier called *self* which will be mapped onto an instance created by *create_temp_inst*, which effectively returns a bound *Env* including *self*. Thus, a copy of the current environment is always contained in *self*. Since *self* is of domain Instance, is has a Ref. When in function evaluation mode, *Ref* = *selfref*, and when in query mode, *self* = current oid under consideration.

Assume that all attribute names are unique. Further, let $A = TR + AD$.

- *getstorage: A →Env →Store →(Env × PostStore)*

  $getstorage[\![A_1, A_2]\!] = \lambda e.\lambda s.$
  let $(e', p) = getstorage[\![A_1]\!]$
  in $check(getstorage[\![A_2]\!]e')(p)$

  $getstorage[\![\text{Aname} : \text{Domain}]\!] = \lambda e.\lambda s.$
  let $(d, p) = D[\![\text{Domain}]\!]s$
  in $((updateenv[\![\text{Aname}]\!]\ d\ e), p)$

getstorage [[Aname=Value]]= $\lambda e.\lambda s.$
let $(d,p) = V[\![Value]\!]s$
in $((updateenv[\![Aname]\!]de), p)$

3. D: *Domain* →*Store* →*(Dv* × *PostStore)*

D[[**integer**]] = $\lambda s.$ **let** $(l,p) = allocate\_locns$
in (in$Integer_locn(l), p)$

D[[**real**]] = $\lambda s.$ **let** $(l,p) = allocate\_locns$
in (in$Real_locn(l), p)$

D[[**string**]] = $\lambda s.$ **let** $(l,p) = allocate\_locns$
in (in$String_locn(l), p)$

$D[\![I]\!] = \lambda s.$ is$Clunction([\![I]\!])$→**let** $(l,p) = allocate\_locns$
in (in$Ref_locn(l), p)$ |(in$Errvalue(), p)$

D[[**tuple**A]] = $\lambda s.$ **let** $(e,p) = getstorage[\![A]\!]empty\_env\ s$
in (in$Tuple_locn(e), p)$

D[[**set**]] = $\lambda s.$ **let** $(l,p) = allocate\_locns$
in (inSet_locn(l),p)

4. V: Value →*Store* →(*Dv* × *PostStore*)

$V[\![Value]\!] = \lambda q.$**cases** $[\![Value]\!]$ *of*
is$Integer(i)$→(in$Integer(i), q)$ |
is$Real(r)$→(in$Real(r), q)$ |
is$String(g)$→(in$String(g), q)$ |
is$Ref(p)$→(in$Ref(p), q)$ |
is$Nil(n)$→$(Null, q)$ |
is$List(l)$→(in$List(l), q)$ |
is$Set(s)$→$(remove_dup(s), q)$ |
is$Tuple(i)$→ **let** $(e,p) = getstorage([\![t]\!]empty\_env\ q)$
in (in$Tuple(e), p)$ |
(in$Errvalue(), q)$

REFERENCES

[1] Agrawal, R., and Gehani, N., "ODE (Object Database and Environment): The Language and Data Model," Proc. ACM SIGMOD, Portland, OR, June 1989.

[2] Alashqur, A., Su, S., and Lam, H., "OQL: A Query Language for Manipulating Object-oriented Databases," 15th Int. Conf. on Very Large Databases, Amsterdam, the Netherlands, August 1989.

[3] Albano, A., Cardelli, L., and Orsini, R., "Galileo: A Strongly Typed Interactive Conceptual Language," ACM TODS, Vol. 10, No. 2, June 1985.

[4] Andrews, T., and Harris, C., "Combining Language and Database Advances in an Object-Oriented Development Environment," Proc. OOPSLA 1987, Orlando, Florida, October 1987.

[5] Atkinson, M.P. and Buneman, O.P., "Types and Persistence in Database Programming Languages," ACM Computing Surveys, Vol. 19, No. 2, June 1987.

[6] Atkinson, M.P., Chisholm, K.P., and Cockshott, W.P., "PS-Algol, an Algol with a Persistent Heap," ACM SIGPLAN Notices, Vol. 17, No. 7, July 1981.

[7] Bancilhon, F., "Query Languages for Object-Oriented Database Systems: Analysis and a Proposal," Proc. of the 4th Int'l Symposium on Databases of Brazil, Campinas, Brazil, April 1989.

[8] Bancilhon, F., Briggs, T., Khoshafian, F., and Valduriez, P., "FAD, A Powerful and Simple Database Language," Proc. 13th VLDB, Brighton, England, September 1987.

[9] Bancilhon, F., and Buneman, P., (eds.), Advances in Database Programming Languages, ACM Press, New York, 1990.

[10] Batory, D., et al., "GENESIS: An Extensible Database Management System," IEEE Trans. on Soft. Engg., Vol. 14, No. 11, 1988.

[11] Beck, H.W., Gala, S.K., and Navathe, S.B., "Classification as a Query Processing Technique in the CANDIDE Semantic Data Model," Proc. of the IEEE International Conf. on Data Engg., Los Angeles, February 1989.

[12] Bloom, T., and Zdonick, S.B., "Issues in the Design of Object-Oriented Database Programming Languages," Proc. OOPSLA, Orlando, Florida, October 1987.

[13] Borgida, A., "Language Features for Flexible Handling of Exceptions in Information Systems," ACM TODS, Vol. 10, No. 4, December 1985.

[14] Brachman, R.J., and Schmolze, J.G., "An overview of the KL-ONE Knowledge Representation System," Cognitive Science, 9, 1985.

[15] Bruce, K., and Wegner, P., "An Algebraic Model of Subtype and Inheritance," Tech. Rep., Dept. of Computer and Information Science, University of Pennsylvania, Philadelphia, 1985.

[16] Buneman, P., and Atkinson, M., "Inheritance and Persistence in Database Programming Languages," Proc. ACM SIGMOD, Washington, D.C., June 1986.

[17] Buneman, P., and Ohori, A., "Polymorphism and Type Inference in Database Programming," unpublished manuscript, Dept. of Computer and Information Science, University of Pennsylvania, Philadelphia, 1990.

[18] Cardelli, L., "A Semantics for Multiple Inheritance," In Semantics of Data Types, G. Kahn, D.B. Macqueen, and G. Plotkin, (eds.), Lecture Notes in Computer Science, Vol. 173, Springer Verlag, New York, 1984.

[19] Cardelli, L., and Wegner, P., "On Understanding Types, Data Abstraction, and Polymorphism," ACM Computing Surveys, Vol. 17, No. 4, December 1985.

[20] Carey, M., DeWitt, D., Richardson, J., and Shekita, E., "The Architecture of the EXODUS Extensible DBMs," Proc. Int. Workshop on Object-Oriented Database Systems, Germany, 1986.

[21] Chakravarthy, U.S., and Nesson, S., "Making an Object-Oriented DBMS Active: Design, Implementation and Evaluation of a Prototype," Proc. of International Conf. on Extended Database Technology, Venice, Italy, March 1990.

[22] Cluet, S., Delobel, C., Lecluse, C., and Richard, P., "Reloop, an Algebra-based Query Language for an Object-Oriented Database System," Proc. IEEE International Conf. on Data Engineering, Kyoto, Japan, February 1987.

[23] Copeland, G., and Maier, D., "Making Smalltalk a Database System," Proc. ACM SIGMOD, New York, 1984.

[24] Courcelle, B., "Fundamental Properties of Infinite Trees," Theoretical Comp. Sc., Vol. 25, 1983.

[25] Elmasri, R., and Navathe, S., Fundamentals of Database Systems, Benjamin/Cummings, Redwood City, California, 1989.

[26] Fishman, D.H., Beech, D., Cate, H.P., "Iris: An Object-Oriented Database System," ACM TOOIS, Vol. 5, No. 1, 1987.

[27] Gallaire, H., Minker, J., and Nicolas, J., "Logic and Databases: a Deductive Approach," ACM Computing Surveys, Vol. 16, No. 2, June 1984.

[28] Hall, P.A.V., "Adding Database Management to Ada," ACM SIGPLAN Notices, Vol. 18, No. 3, April 1983.

[29] Harper, R., Milner, R., and Tofte, M., "The Definition of Standard ML (version 2)," LFCS Report, ECS-LFCS-88-62, Dept. of Computer Sc., University of Edinburgh, Scotland, August 1988.

[30] Hull, R. and King, R., "Semantic Database Modeling: Survey, Applications, and Research Issues," ACM Computing Surveys, Vol. 19, No. 3, September 1987.

[31] Jagadish, H.V., "Incorporating Hierarchy in Relational Model of Data," Proc. ACM SIGMOD, Portland, Oregon, May 1989.

[32] Khoshafian, S., and Copeland, G., "Object Identity," Proc. First OOPSLA Conf., Portland, Oregon, September 1986.

[33] Kifer, M., and Lausen, G., "F-Logic: A Higher Order Language for Reasoning about Objects, Inheritance and Schemes," Proc. of the ACM SIGMOD, Portland, Oregon, June 1989. 1989.

[34] Koch, J., Mall, M., Putfarken, P., Reimer, M., Schmidt, J.W., and Zehnder, C.A., "Modula/R Report, Lilith Version," Technical Report, ETH, Zurich, Switzerland, 1983.

[35] Lecluse, C., Richard, P., and Velez, F., "O_2, an Object-Oriented Data Model," Proc. ACM SIGMOD, Chicago, June 1988.

[36] MacGregor, R.M., "ARIEL—A Semantic Front-end to Relational DBMSs," Proc. VLDB, Stockholm, August 1985.

[37] Maier, D., Stein, J., Otis, A., and Purdy, A., "Development of Object-oriented DBMS," ACM SIGPLAN Notices, Vol. 21, No. 11, November 1986.

[38] Manola, F., and Dayal, U., "PDM: An Object-Oriented Data Model," Proc. Int. Workshop on Object-Oriented Database Systems, Asilomar, California, September 1986.

[39] McCarthy, D.R., and Dayal, U., "The Architecture of an Active, Object-Oriented Database System," Proc. ACM SIGMOD, Portland, Oregon, June 1989.

[40] Morgenstern, M., "Active Databases as a Paradigm for Enhanced Computing Environments," Proc. 9th VLDB, August 1983.

[41] Mylopoulos, J., Bernstein, P.A., and Wong, H.K.T., "A Language Facility for Designing Database Intensive Applications," ACM TODS, Vol. 5, No. 2, June 1980.

[42] Nebel, Bernhard, "Computational Complexity of Terminological Reasoning in BACK," Artificial Intelligence, Vol. 34, No. 3, 1988.

[43] Ohori, A., Buneman, P., and Breazu-Tannen, V., "Database Programming in Machiavelli—A Polymorphic Language with Static Type Inferencing," Proc. ACM SIGMOD Conf., Portland, Oregon, 1989.

[44] Ontologic, Inc., "ONTOS Object Database Documentation," Release 1.5, Burlington, Massachussetts, 1989.

[45] Patel-Schneider, P.F., "Small can be Beautiful in Knowledge Representation," FLAIR Technical Report 37, Fairchild, Inc., Austin Texas, 1984.

[46] Rowe, L.A., and Stonebraker, M.R., "The POSTGRES Data Model," Proc. 13th VLDB, Brighton, England, September 1987.

[47] Schmidt, D.A., Denotational Semantics, Wm. C. Brown, Dubuque, Iowa, 1985.

[48] Schmidt, J.W., "Some High-level Language Constructs for Data of Type Relation," ACM TODS, Vol. 2, No. 3, September 1977.

[49] Schwartz, J.T., Dewar, R.B.K., Dubinsky, E., and Schonberg, E., "Programming with Sets: An Introduction to SETL," Springer-Verlag, Berlin, 1986.

[50] Shaw, G.M., and Zdonick, S.B., "An Object-Oriented Query Algebra," Proc. of Second Int. Workshop on Database Programming Languages, August 1989.

[51] Shipman, D., "The Functional Data Model and the Data Language DAPLEX," ACM TODS, Vol. 12, No. 3, March 1981.

[52] Smith, J.M., Fox, S., and Landers, T., "ADAPLEX: Rationale and Reference Manual," 2d ed., CCA, Cambridge, Massachussetts.

[53] Straube, D., and Tamer Ozsu, M., "Type Consistency of Queries in an Object-Oriented System," Proc. Joint ACM OOPSLA/ECOOP Conf. on Object-Oriented Programming, October 1990.

[54] Wand, M., "Type Inference for Records Concatenation and Simple Objects," Proc. Fourth IEEE Symp. on Logic in Computer Science, 1989.

[55] Widom, J., and Finkelstein, S., "Set-Oriented Production Rules in Relational Database Systems," Proc. ACM SIGMOD, Atlantic City, New Jersey, May 1990.

[56] Yu, L., and Osborn, S., "An Evaluation Framework for Algebraic Object-Oriented Query Models," Proc. IEEE International Conf. on Data Engineering, Kyoto, Japan, April 1991.

[57] Zaniolo, C., "The Database Language GEM," Proc. ACM SIGMOD, June 1983.

BIOGRAPHICAL SKETCH

Sunit Kalyanji Gala was born on January 24, 1964, in Bombay, India. He received his undergraduate degree in Instrumentation from Birla Institute of Technology and Science, India, in June, 1985. He received his Master of Science degree in December 1987 and his Doctor of Philosophy degree in December 1991 from the University of Florida, Gainesville. His current research interests are database programming languages, database applications of programming language theory, type algebras and query algebras.

I certify that I have read this study and that in my opinion it conforms to acceptable standards of scholarly presentation and is fully adequate, in scope and quality, as a dissertation for the degree of Doctor of Philosophy.

Shamkant B. Navathe, Chair
Professor of Computer and
Information Sciences

I certify that I have read this study and that in my opinion it conforms to acceptable standards of scholarly presentation and is fully adequate, in scope and quality, as a dissertation for the degree of Doctor of Philosophy.

Manuel E. Bermudez
Associate Professor of Computer and
Information Sciences

I certify that I have read this study and that in my opinion it conforms to acceptable standards of scholarly presentation and is fully adequate, in scope and quality, as a dissertation for the degree of Doctor of Philosophy.

Herman Lam
Associate Professor of Electrical
Engineering

I certify that I have read this study and that in my opinion it conforms to acceptable standards of scholarly presentation and is fully adequate, in scope and quality, as a dissertation for the degree of Doctor of Philosophy.

Richard Newman-Wolfe
Assistant Professor of Computer and
Information Sciences

I certify that I have read this study and that in my opinion it conforms to acceptable standards of scholarly presentation and is fully adequate, in scope and quality, as a dissertation for the degree of Doctor of Philosophy.

José C. Principe
Associate Professor of Electrical Engineering

I certify that I have read this study and that in my opinion it conforms to acceptable standards of scholarly presentation and is fully adequate, in scope and quality, as a dissertation for the degree of Doctor of Philosophy.

Stanley Y. W. Su
Professor of Electrical Engineering

This dissertation was submitted to the Graduate Faculty of the College of Engineering and to the Graduate School and was accepted as partial fulfillment of the requirements for the degree of Doctor of Philosophy.

December 1991.

Herbert A. Bevis
for Winfred M. Phillips
Dean, College of Engineering

Madelyn M. Lockhart
Dean, Graduate School

www.ingramcontent.com/pod-product-compliance
Lightning Source LLC
Chambersburg PA
CBHW080430060326
40689CB00019B/4448

* 9 7 8 0 5 3 0 0 0 5 6 2 1 *